fuss-free entertaining
with just 4 ingredients

fuss-free entertaining with just 4 ingredients

60 amazingly delicious step-by-step recipes for parties and special occasions using only four ingredients – guaranteed to impress your family and friends

Contributing editor Joanna Farrow

southwater

This edition is published by Southwater

Southwater is an imprint of Anness Publishing Ltd
Hermes House, 88–89 Blackfriars Road, London SE1 8HA
tel. 020 7401 2077; fax 020 7633 9499
www.southwaterbooks.com; info@anness.com

UK agent: The Manning Partnership Ltd
6 The Old Dairy, Melcombe Road,Bath BA2 3LR
tel. 01225 478444; fax 01225 478440
sales@manning-partnership.co.uk

UK distributor: Grantham Book Services Ltd
Isaac Newton Way, Alma Park Industrial Estate
Grantham, Lincs NG31 9SD
tel. 01476 541080; fax 01476 541061
orders@gbs.tbs-ltd.co.uk

North American agent/distributor: National Book Network
4501 Forbes Boulevard, Suite 200, Lanham, MD 20706
tel. 301 459 3366; fax 301 429 5746
www.nbnbooks.com

Australian agent/distributor: Pan Macmillan Australia
Level 18, St Martins Tower, 31 Market St, Sydney, NSW 2000
tel. 1300 135 113; fax 1300 135 103
customer.service@macmillan.com.au

New Zealand agent/distributor: David Bateman Ltd
30 Tarndale Grove, Off Bush Road, Albany, Auckland
tel. (09) 415 7664; fax (09) 415 8892

A CIP catalogue record for this book is available from the British Library.

Publisher: Joanna Lorenz
Editorial Director: Judith Simons
Editors: Susannah Blake, Bridget Jones and Elizabeth Woodland
Cover Designer: Balley Design Associates
Photography: Tim Auty, Martin Brigdale, Nicky Dowey, Gus Filgate, Michelle Garrett, Amanda Heywood, William Lingwood, Craig Robertson and Simon Smith
Recipes: Alex Barker, Jacqueline Clark, Joanna Farrow, Brian Glover, Jane Milton, Jennie Shapter, Marlena Spieler and Kate Whiteman
Production Controller: Pedro Nelson

1 3 5 7 9 10 8 6 4 2

Material from this book has previously been published in *Take Four*

NOTES

Bracketed terms are intended for American readers.

For all recipes, quantities are given in both metric and imperial measures and, where appropriate, measures are also given in standard cups and spoons. Follow one set, but not a mixture, because they are not interchangeable.

Standard spoon and cup measures are level.

1 tsp = 5ml, 1 tbsp = 15ml, 1 cup = 250ml/8fl oz

Australian standard tablespoons are 20ml. Australian readers should use 3 tsp in place of 1 tbsp for measuring small quantities of gelatine, flour, salt, etc.

Medium (US large) eggs are used unless otherwise stated.

The very young, elderly and those in ill-health or with a compromised immune system are advised against consuming raw eggs or dishes containing raw eggs.

Front cover shows Spicy Chickpea Samosas – for recipe, see page 21.

Contents

Entertaining with Four Ingredients

In recent years, cooking and eating trends have changed considerably, with more emphasis on dishes that are quick and easy to prepare, yet that are still exciting, sophisticated and delicious. This book teaches you how to really make the most of food – with simple, fabulous recipes that use only four ingredients, or less. The aim of this book is to provide a wealth of ideas and advice for creating successful dinner parties for every occasion, and also allows for fuss-free preparation, giving you more time to sit back, relax and enjoy the company of your friends and family.

When you're cooking with four ingredients, each one has to be a star player. It is important to buy the best quality ingredients you can find so be selective when buying, as the better the raw materials, the more flavour the finished dish will have. Top-quality produce will also need fewer additional seasonings or flavourings to make it taste fabulous. Buying the best does not necessarily mean paying more. For example meat from a good, traditional-style butcher is often cheaper than the better-quality types in the supermarket and it will probably have a fuller flavour. Good fish can be slightly harder to find. Be particularly choosy when buying from supermarket fish counters: avoid tired-looking specimens and remember that it is better to go for good-quality frozen fish and shellfish rather than poor-quality fresh. Farmers' market stores can be great sources of good-quality fruit and vegetables, often at a good price, even for the more unusual produce.

Ready-made stocks and sauces are infinitely useful for creating quick and easy meals and are a great way to cut down on preparation and cooking time. A basic tomato sauce can lay the foundations for hundreds of different dishes such as stews, casseroles and pasta. Simply add poultry, meat, fish, vegetables or pulses and flavour with fresh herbs and spices. Sauces such as pesto are great for adding flavour, while a really great ready-made custard can be the perfect base for an ice cream. Good-quality bought sauces are readily available fresh or in jars – check out the list of ingredients on the label for some indication of the quality. A good bought liquid concentrate or fresh stock is worth keeping in the refrigerator or freezer. Remember that many bought chilled fresh products are suitable for home freezing, which is a good way of extending their shelf life. Alternatively, you can make your own supply of basic stocks and sauces and freeze them in practical, ready-to-use batches.

Choosing really fresh, good-quality ingredients will help you to create delicious, flavoursome dishes.

Fresh herbs go perfectly with other simple flavours and play an essential role in fuss-free cooking.

Fresh fruit forms the basis for a wonderful range of simple, yet elegant desserts.

Storecupboard essentials

Try to avoid overstocking the storecupboard (pantry). Choose good-quality extra virgin olive oil and balsamic vinegar for dressings and a lighter oil such as sunflower oil for cooking. A nut oil such as walnut or hazelnut is an interesting alternative to olive oil in salad dressings. One or two flavoured oils are great for adding extra taste.

Preserved or dried vegetables such as sun-dried tomatoes, bottled roasted (bell) peppers and capers have a powerful taste and can be useful for boosting flavour in many Mediterranean-style dishes. Dried mushrooms bring a full flavour to mushroom dishes and can be good for perking up simple soups, stews, casseroles and risottos.

Keep herb and spice supplies to a minimum as both lose their flavour comparatively quickly, particularly if exposed to light and warmth. If possible, it is better to grow or buy fresh herbs and freeze any leftovers for future use rather than stocking a collection full of dried spices that have an inferior flavour. If possible, stock whole spices such as cumin and coriander and grind them using a mortar and pestle or in a spice grinder as required, as ground spices tend to lose their flavour quickly. Freshly grated whole nutmeg is better than ready ground and it adds interest to potato dishes and white sauces.

Other items you should keep in stock include salt and black peppercorns, sugar, plain (all-purpose) flour and cornflour (cornstarch), plus basic staples such as pasta and rice. It is also handy to have a small selection of condiments or sauces such as soy sauce or pesto that can help to perk up or enhance the flavour of simple dishes.

Keep a selection of flavoured oils in the storecupboard. They can be used as a simple dressing for freshly cooked pasta or salad.

Using the recipes

Each recipe uses no more than four ingredients, excluding salt, pepper and water. Some recipes use ready-made stock or sauce – but you can always use a homemade one if you prefer. Serving suggestions and ideas for garnishes or decorations are included where appropriate, but these are not essential for the success of the dish. There are also suggestions for variations that offer alternative or additional flavourings and handy cook's tips that will help you achieve successful results every time.

Making Basic Stocks

A well-flavoured stock is particularly good in dishes that rely on minimal ingredients. Good-quality ready-made stocks – either cube, powders or liquid concentrate – are readily available but stocks are easy and cheap to make. Always ask for the meat bones when buying from a butcher and trimmings if you have fish prepared by the fishmonger as these are perfect for making good stock. A chicken carcass from a roast makes excellent stock, particularly if you've packed it with herbs, onions, garlic or other aromatics before roasting. A good vegetable stock can be made from trimmings when preparing vegetables and small quantities of leftover produce. Leave the onion skins on if you want a rich, dark-coloured stock.

Beef Stock MAKES ABOUT 1 LITRE/1¾ PINTS/4 CUPS

900g/2lb beef bones

2 unpeeled onions, quartered

1 bouquet garni

2 large carrots, roughly chopped

1 Preheat the oven to 220°C/425°F/Gas 7. Put the beef bones in a roasting pan and roast for about 45 minutes, or until well browned.

2 Transfer the roasted bones to a large, heavy pan. Add the onion quarters, leaving the skins on, the bouquet garni and chopped carrots. Add 5ml/1 tsp salt and 5ml/1 tsp black peppercorns. Pour over about 1.7 litres/3 pints/7½ cups cold water and bring just to the boil.

3 Using a slotted spoon, skim off any scum on the surface of the stock. Reduce the heat and partially cover the pan. Simmer the stock on the lowest heat for about 3 hours, then set aside to cool slightly.

4 Strain the stock into a large bowl and leave to cool completely, then remove any fat from the surface. Store the stock in the refrigerator for up to 3 days or freeze for up to 6 months.

Chicken Stock MAKES ABOUT 1 LITRE/1¾ PINTS/4 CUPS

1 large roast chicken carcass

2 unpeeled onions, quartered

3 bay leaves

2 large carrots, roughly chopped

1 Put the chicken carcass and any loose bones and roasting juices into a heavy pan in which they fit snugly. Add the onion quarters, bay leaves and chopped carrots.

2 Add 2.5ml/½ tsp salt and 5ml/1 tsp black peppercorns to the pan, and pour over 1.7 litres/3 pints/7½ cups cold water. Bring just to the boil.

3 Reduce the heat, partially cover the pan and cook on the lowest setting for about 1½ hours. Using a large spoon, carefully turn the chicken in the stock and crush the carcass occasionally.

4 Leave the stock to cool slightly, then strain into a large bowl and leave to cool completely. When cool, remove any fat from the surface. Store the stock in the refrigerator for up to 2 days or freeze for up to 6 months.

Fish Stock MAKES ABOUT 600ML/1 PINT/2½ CUPS

500g/1¼ lb fish bones and trimmings, without heads and gills

1 bouquet garni

1 onion or 3–4 shallots, peeled and quartered

2 celery sticks, roughly chopped

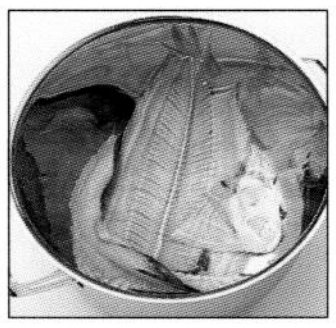

1 Pack the fish bones and trimmings into a heavy pan and add the bouquet garni, quartered onion or shallots and celery.

2 Add 2.5ml/½ tsp salt and 2.5ml/½ tsp peppercorns to the pan and pour over 1 litre/1¾ pints/4 cups water. Bring to the boil.

3 Reduce the heat, partially cover the pan and cook on the lowest setting for about 30 minutes, stirring occasionally. Leave to cool slightly, then strain into a bowl and cool completely. Store in the refrigerator for up to 24 hours or freeze for up to 3 months.

Vegetable Stock MAKES ABOUT 1 LITRE/1¾ PINTS/4 CUPS

3 unpeeled onions, quartered

200g/7oz large open mushrooms

300–400g/11–14oz mixed vegetables, such as broccoli, carrots, celery, tomatoes and/or spring onions (scallions), roughly chopped

45ml/3 tbsp green or brown lentils

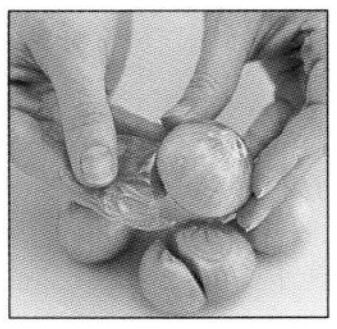

1 Place the onions in a heavy pan with the mushrooms, mixed vegetables and green or brown lentils.

2 Add 2.5ml/½ tsp salt, 10ml/2 tsp peppercorns and 1.7 litres/3 pints/7½ cups water to the pan. Bring to the boil, then reduce the heat and simmer, partially covered, for 50–60 minutes.

3 Leave the stock to cool slightly, then strain into a bowl and leave to cool. Store in the refrigerator for up to 24 hours or freeze for up to 6 months.

Bouquet Garni

This little bundle of herbs is perfect for adding flavour to stocks, soups and stews. Tying the herbs in a bundle means that the bouquet garni is easy to remove after cooking. A traditional bouquet garni comprises sprigs of parsley, thyme and a bay leaf, but you can vary the herbs according to the dish and/or main ingredients. Rosemary and oregano are good with lamb, while mint, chervil, basil, chives and tarragon go well with fish.

1 Using a short length of string, tie together a bay leaf and sprigs of thyme and parsley.

2 Alternatively, place the herbs in the centre of a square of muslin (cheesecloth) and tie into a neat bundle using a short length of string.

3 Use the bouquet garni immediately or freeze, ready for cooking. (Herbs tied in muslin are better suited to freezing than bundles simply tied with string.)

FREEZING STOCK

The main ingredients for stock can be frozen – meat bones, fish trimmings or a cooked chicken carcass – ready to make home-made stock at a later date.

More conveniently, stock itself freezes very well. Once the stock has been strained and the fat removed, reduce the volume by boiling the stock uncovered. This concentrates its flavour and takes up less freezer space. A highly reduced stock, boiled to a thick syrup, can be frozen in an ice cube tray. Make a note of the volume before boiling, then add this to the label when packing the stock for the freezer. This way you will know how much water to add when the concentrated stock is thawed.

Making Basic Savoury Sauces

A good sauce can provide the finishing touch for a dish. There are a large number of ready-made sauces available, but they are also very easy to make yourself. One of the most basic sauces is the classic savoury white sauce, which can be served as a simple topping for vegetables or flavoured with additional ingredients such as cheese and herbs. A basic fresh tomato sauce is widely used for pasta dishes, pizza toppings and vegetable dishes. Hollandaise sauce is another classic accompaniment for fish and vegetables.

White Sauce MAKES ABOUT 300ML/½ PINT/1¼ CUPS

300ml/½ pint/1¼ cups milk

15g/½oz/1 tbsp butter

15g/½oz plain (all-purpose) flour

freshly grated nutmeg

1 Warm the milk in a small pan. In a separate pan, melt the butter over a gently heat, then add the flour and cook, stirring, for 1 minute until the mixture forms a thick paste. Remove the pan from the heat and gradually add the warmed milk, whisking continuously until smooth.

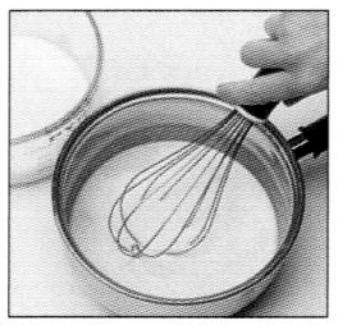

2 Return the pan to a gentle heat and cook, whisking, until the sauce boils, is smooth and thickened. Season with salt and freshly ground pepper and plenty of nutmeg.

Fresh Tomato Sauce MAKES ABOUT 1 LITRE/1¾ PINTS/4 CUPS

1.3kg/3lb ripe tomatoes

120ml/4fl oz/½ cup garlic-infused olive oil

1 large onion, finely chopped

small handful of basil leaves, torn, or 30ml/2 tbsp chopped fresh oregano

1 Put the tomatoes in a bowl, pour over boiling water to cover and leave to stand for about 1 minute until the skins split. Drain and peel, then roughly chop the flesh.

2 Heat half the oil in a large heavy pan. Add the chopped onion and cook gently for about 3 minutes, or until softened but not browned. Add the tomatoes and the remaining oil to the pan and cook gently, stirring, for 5 minutes, or until the tomatoes are soft and juicy. Add the herbs, cover and cook gently for 20–25 minutes, stirring frequently, until the sauce is thickened and pulpy. Season to taste.

Hollandaise Sauce MAKES ABOUT 120ML/4FL OZ/½ CUP

45ml/3 tbsp white wine or herb-infused vinegar

1 bay leaf

2 egg yolks

115g/4oz/½ cup butter, chilled

1 Put the vinegar in a small pan with the bay leaf and add 5ml/1 tsp black peppercorns. Boil rapidly until reduced to 15ml/1 tsp, then strain into a heatproof bowl. Put in a clean pan, add the egg yolks and a little salt and whisk lightly until thoroughly combined. Cut the chilled butter into small pieces.

2 Add the butter to the pan and set the pan over a very low heat. Whisk continuously so that as the butter melts it is blended into the egg yolks. When all the butter has melted, continue whisking until the sauce is thick and smooth.

3 Season the sauce with salt and ground black pepper to taste, adding a few extra drops of vinegar, if you like, to give a slightly tangy flavour. Serve warm.

Making Basic Sweet Sauces

From creamy, comforting custard to an elegant fruit coulis, sweet sauces can be used to uplift the simplest puddings and desserts to create a truly spectacular dish. They can be served as an accompaniment or make up an intrinsic part of a dish. These sweet sauces rely on just a few basic ingredients and minimal effort, producing irresistible results. The dessert sauce can be made in advance, before serving the meal, ready for reheating or serving cold. Even custard can be re-heated, just take care to use very gentle heat to prevent it from curdling.

Real Custard MAKES 300ML/½ PINT/1¼ CUPS

300ml/½ pint/1¼ cups full-cream (whole) milk or half milk and half double (heavy) cream

3 egg yolks

5ml/1 tsp cornflour (cornstarch)

45ml/3 tbsp caster (superfine) sugar or vanilla sugar

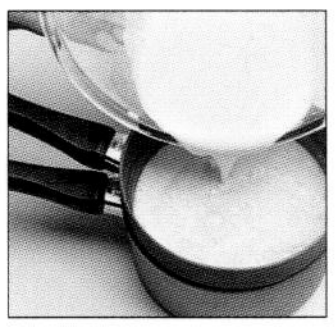

1 Pour the milk or milk and cream mixture into a double boiler or heavy pan and bring slowly to the boil over a very gentle heat.

2 Meanwhile, whisk the egg yolks with the cornflour and sugar until thoroughly mixed. Pour the boiled milk into the yolk mixture, whisking continuously until combined.

3 Pour the mixture back into the cleaned pan and cook over the lowest heat, stirring continuously with a wooden spoon, for 8–10 minutes, or until the mixture coats the back of the spoon. Immediately pour the custard through a sieve (strainer) into a bowl or jug (pitcher) to prevent it from overcooking. Serve warm.

Summer Fruit Coulis MAKES ABOUT 250ML/8FL OZ/1 CUP

130g/4½oz raspberries

130g/4½oz strawberries

10–15ml/2–3 tsp icing (confectioners') sugar

15ml/1 tbsp orange liqueur or Kirsch (optional)

1 Place the raspberries and strawberries in a food processor and process until smooth. Press the mixture through a fine strainer set over a bowl to remove the tiny seeds.

2 Return the strained fruit purée to the food processor or blender and add 10ml/2 tsp of the icing sugar with the orange liqueur or Kirsch, if using, and process briefly until well combined. Check the sweetness of the coulis, then add a little more icing sugar if necessary and process again to mix.

Rich Chocolate Sauce MAKES ABOUT 250ML/8FL OZ/1 CUP

130g/4½oz caster (superfine) sugar

175g/6oz plain (semisweet) chocolate, broken into pieces

25g/1oz/2 tbsp unsalted (sweet) butter

30ml/2 tbsp brandy or coffee liqueur (optional)

1 Put the sugar in a small heavy pan with 120ml/4fl oz/½ cup water and heat gently until the sugar dissolves. Bring to the boil and boil for 1 minute.

2 Remove from the heat and stir in the chocolate and butter, stirring until the chocolate has melted and the sauce is smooth. Stir in the brandy or coffee liqueur, if using, and serve warm.

Buffet, Finger Food and Dips

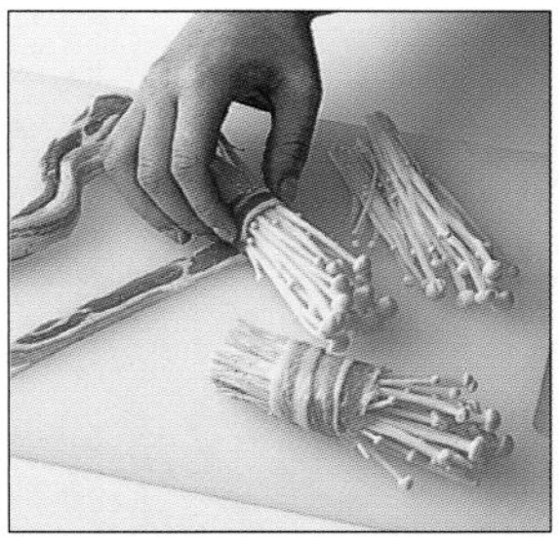

Here is a collection of stylish little bites to satisfy your party guests. Whether you're just having a few friends over for drinks, or a large gathering, you'll find just what you need here.

Spanish Salted Almonds

Served with a glass of chilled dry sherry, these delicious salted nuts make a perfect tapas dish or pre-dinner snack.

SERVES FOUR TO SIX

1 egg white

200g/7oz/generous 1 cup shelled unblanched almonds

a good handful of flaked sea salt

1 Preheat the oven 200°C/400°F/Gas 6. Whisk the egg white in a bowl until it forms stiff peaks.

2 Add the almonds to the egg white, and stir until the nuts are thoroughly coated. Turn the mixture on to a baking sheet and spread out evenly in a single layer.

3 Sprinkle the salt over the almonds and bake for about 15 minutes, or until the egg white and salt are crusty. Leave to cool completely, then serve in bowls with a selection of other nibbles, dips and pâtés.

Polenta Chips

These tasty Parmesan-flavoured batons are best served warm from the oven with a spicy, tangy dip. A bowl of Thai chilli dipping sauce or a creamy, chilli-spiked guacamole are perfect for dipping into.

MAKES ABOUT EIGHTY

1 Put 1.5 litres/2½ pints/6¼ cups water into a large heavy pan and bring to the boil. Reduce the heat, add the salt and pour in the polenta in a steady stream, stirring constantly with a wooden spoon. Cook over a low heat for about 5 minutes, stirring, until the mixture thickens and comes away from the sides of the pan.

2 Remove the pan from the heat and add the cheese, butter and pepper. Add more salt if needed, and stir until smooth. Pour on to a smooth surface, such as a marble slab or a baking sheet.

3 Using a metal spatula, spread out the polenta to a thickness of 2cm/¾in and shape into a rectangle. Leave to stand for at least 30 minutes until cold. Meanwhile preheat the oven to 200°C/400°F/Gas 6 and lightly oil two or three baking sheets.

4 Cut the polenta slab in half, then carefully cut into even-size strips. Bake for 40–50 minutes, or until dark golden brown and crunchy, turning from time to time. Serve warm.

10ml/2 tsp salt, plus extra to taste

375g/13oz/3¼ cups quick-cook polenta

150g/5oz/1½ cups freshly grated Parmesan cheese

90g/3½oz/7 tbsp butter

10ml/2 tsp cracked black pepper

olive oil, for brushing

Brandade of Salt Cod

There are many versions of this creamy French salt cod purée: some contain mashed potatoes, others truffles. Serve the brandade with warmed crispbread or crusty bread for a tasty appetizer, or as part of a buffet. You can omit the garlic from the brandade, if you prefer, and serve toasted slices of French bread rubbed with garlic instead.

SERVES SIX

200g/7oz salt cod

250ml/8fl oz/1 cup extra virgin olive oil

4 garlic cloves, crushed

250ml/8fl oz/1 cup double (heavy) or whipping cream

1 Soak the fish in cold water for 24 hours, changing the water frequently. Drain the fish well. Cut the fish into pieces, place in a shallow pan and pour in enough cold water to cover. Heat the water until it is simmering and poach the fish for 8 minutes, until it is just cooked. Drain the fish, then remove the skin and bones.

2 Combine the extra virgin olive oil and crushed garlic cloves in a small pan and heat gently. In another pan, heat the double cream until it just starts to simmer.

3 Put the cod into a food processor, process it briefly, then gradually add alternate amounts of the garlic-flavoured olive oil and cream, while continuing to process the mixture. The aim is to create a purée with the consistency of mashed potato.

4 Season to taste with freshly ground black pepper, then scoop the brandade into a serving bowl or on to individual serving plates and serve with crispbread or crusty bread.

Baba Ghanoush

Adjust the amount of aubergine, garlic and lemon juice in this richly flavoured Middle Eastern aubergine dip depending on how creamy, garlicky or tart you want it to be. The dip can served with a garnish of chopped fresh coriander leaves, olives or pickled cucumbers. Hot pepper sauce or a little ground coriander can be added, too.

SERVES TWO TO FOUR

1 large or 2 medium aubergines (eggplants)

2–4 garlic cloves, chopped

90–150ml/6–10 tbsp tahini

juice of 1 lemon, or to taste

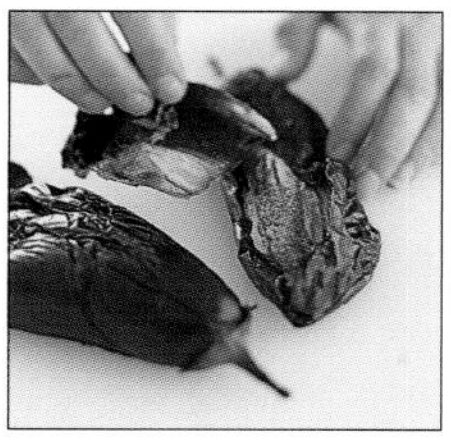

1 Place the aubergine(s) directly over the flame of a gas stove or on the coals of a barbecue. Turn the aubergine(s) fairly frequently until deflated and the skin is evenly charred. Remove from the heat with tongs. Alternatively, place under a hot grill (broiler), turning frequently, until charred.

2 Put the aubergine(s) in a plastic bag and seal the top tightly, or place in a bowl and cover with crumpled kitchen paper. Leave to cool for 30–60 minutes.

3 Peel off the blackened skin from the aubergine(s), reserving the juices. Chop the aubergine flesh, either by hand for a coarse texture or in a food processor for a smooth purée. Put the aubergine in a bowl and stir in the reserved juices.

4 Add the garlic and tahini to the aubergine and stir until smooth. Stir in the lemon juice. If the mixture becomes too thick, add 15–30ml/1–2 tbsp water. Season with salt and ground black pepper to taste and spoon into a serving bowl. Serve at room temperature.

Egg and Onion Topping

This dish is delicious served sprinkled with chopped parsley and onion rings on crackers, piled on toast, or used as a sandwich or bagel filling. Serve as part of a buffet with a selection of dips and toppings.

SERVES FOUR TO SIX

8–10 eggs

6–8 spring onions (scallions) and/or 1 yellow or white onion, very finely chopped, plus extra to garnish

60–90ml/4–6 tbsp mayonnaise or rendered chicken fat

mild French wholegrain mustard, to taste (optional if using mayonnaise)

1 Put the eggs in a large pan and cover with cold water. Bring the water to the boil and when it boils, reduce the heat and simmer over a low heat for 10 minutes.

2 Place the boiled eggs in a strainer and cool them under cold running water. When cool, remove the shells from the eggs and discard. Dry the eggs and chop coarsely.

3 Place the chopped eggs in a large bowl, add the onions, season generously with salt and black pepper and mix well. Add enough mayonnaise or chicken fat to bind the mixture together. Stir in the mustard, if using, and chill before serving.

COOK'S TIP

The amount of rendered chicken fat or mayonnaise required will depend on how much onion you use in this dish.

Cheese with Green Olives

This dish is flavoured with piquant green olives, are served with drinks and little crackers or toast – spread generously on chunks of fresh, crusty bread or bagels.

SERVES FOUR

175–200g/6–7oz soft white (farmer's) cheese

65g/2½oz feta cheese, preferably sheep's milk, lightly crumbled

20–30 pitted green olives, some chopped, the rest halved or quartered

2–3 large pinches of fresh thyme, plus extra to garnish

1 Place the soft white cheese in a mixing bowl and stir with the back of a spoon or a fork until soft and smooth. Add the crumbled feta cheese and stir the two cheeses together until they are thoroughly combined.

2 Add the chopped, halved and quartered olives and the pinches of fresh thyme to the cheese mixture and mix thoroughly.

3 Spoon the mixture into a bowl, sprinkle with thyme and serve with crackers, toast, chunks of bread or bagels.

Bacon-rolled Enokitake Mushrooms

The Japanese name for this dish is *Obimaki enoki*: an *obi* (belt or sash) is made from bacon and wrapped around enokitake mushrooms before they are grilled. The strong, smoky flavour of the bacon complements the subtle flavour of mushrooms. Small heaps of ground white pepper can be offered with these savouries, if you like.

SERVES FOUR

450g/1lb fresh enokitake mushrooms

6 rindless smoked streaky (fatty) bacon rashers (strips)

4 lemon wedges

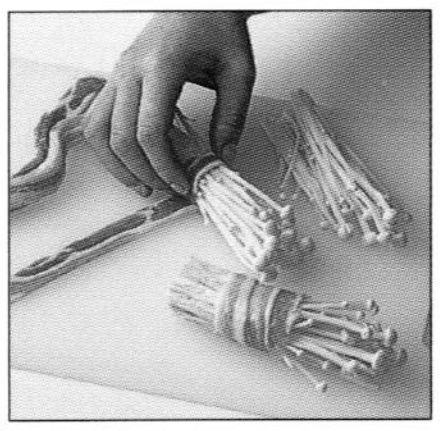

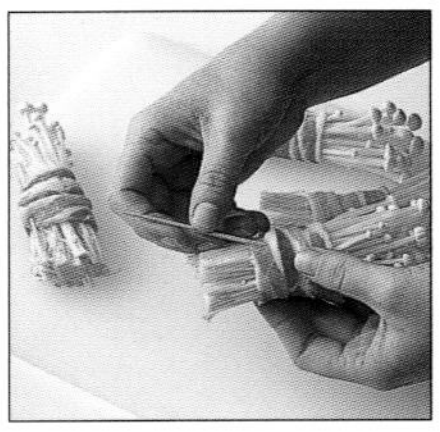

1 Cut off the root part of each enokitake cluster 2cm/¾in from the end. Do not separate the stems. Cut the bacon rashers in half lengthways.

2 Divide the enokitake into 12 equal bunches. Take one bunch, then place the middle of the enokitake near the edge of one bacon rasher, with 2.5–4cm/1–1½in of enokitake protruding at each end.

3 Carefully roll up the bunch of enokitake in the bacon. Tuck any straying short stems into the bacon and slide the bacon slightly upwards at each roll to cover about 4cm/1½in of the enokitake. Secure the end of the bacon roll with a cocktail stick (toothpick). Repeat using the remaining enokitake and bacon to make 11 more rolls.

4 Preheat the grill (broiler) to high. Place the enokitake rolls on an oiled wire rack. Grill (broil) both sides until the bacon is crisp and the enokitake start to char. This takes 10–13 minutes.

5 Remove the enokitake rolls and place on a board. Using a fork and knife, chop each roll in half in the middle of the bacon belt. Arrange the top part of the enokitake roll standing upright, the bottom part lying down next to it. Add a wedge of lemon to each portion and serve.

Spicy Chickpea Samosas

A blend of crushed chickpeas and coriander sauce makes an interesting alternative to the more familiar meat or vegetable fillings in these little pastries. The samosas look pretty garnished with fresh coriander leaves and finely sliced onion and are delicious served with a simple dip made from Greek (US strained plain) yogurt and chopped fresh mint leaves.

MAKES EIGHTEEN

1 Preheat the oven to 220°C/425°F/Gas 7. Process half the chickpeas to a paste in a food processor. Scoop the paste into a bowl and add the whole chickpeas, the hara masala or coriander sauce, and season with salt and pepper. Mix until well combined.

2 Lay a sheet of filo pastry on a work surface and cut into three strips. Brush the strips with a little of the oil. Place a dessertspoon of the filling at one end of a strip. Turn one corner diagonally over the filling to meet the long edge. Continue folding the filling and the pastry along the length of the strip, keeping the triangular shape. Transfer to a baking sheet and repeat with the remaining filling and pastry.

3 Brush the pastries with any remaining oil and bake for 15 minutes, until the pastry is golden. Cool slightly before serving.

2 x 400g/14oz cans chickpeas, drained and rinsed

120ml/4fl oz/½ cup hara masala or coriander (cilantro) sauce

275g/10oz filo pastry

60ml/4 tbsp chilli and garlic oil

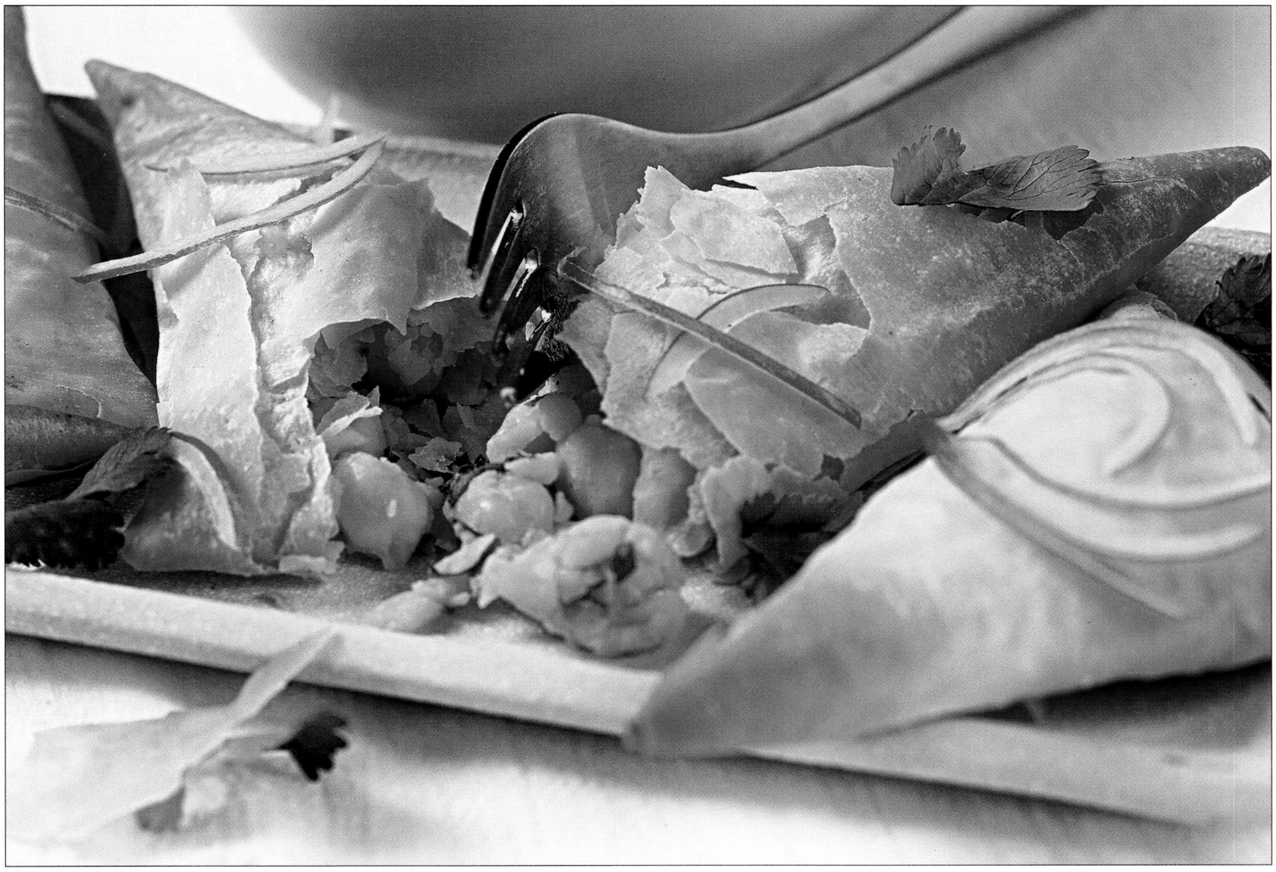

Red Onion and Olive Pissaladière

For a taste of the Mediterranean, try this French-style pizza – it makes a delicious addition to the buffet table. Cook the sliced red onions slowly until they are caramelized and sweet before piling them into the pastry cases. To prepare the recipe in advance, pile the cooled onions on to the pastry round and chill the pissaladière until you are ready to bake it.

SERVES SIX

75ml/5 tbsp extra virgin olive oil

500g/1¼lb small red onions, thinly sliced

500g/1¼lb puff pastry, thawed if frozen

75g/3oz/¾ cup small pitted black olives

1 Preheat the oven to 220°C/425°F/Gas 7. Heat the oil in a large, heavy frying pan and cook the onions gently, stirring frequently, for 15–20 minutes, until they are soft and golden. Season to taste.

2 Roll out the pastry thinly on a floured surface. Cut out a 33cm/13in round and transfer it to a lightly dampened baking sheet.

3 Spread the onions over the pastry in an even layer to within 1cm/½in of the edge. Sprinkle the olives on top. Bake the tart for 20–25 minutes, until the pastry is risen and deep golden. Cut into wedges and serve warm.

Potato and Onion Tortilla

This deep-set omelette with sliced potatoes and onions is the best-known Spanish tortilla and they are ideal for buffets. Tortilla are often made with a variety of ingredients – chopped red or yellow (bell) peppers, cooked peas, or grated cheese can all be added to the mixture in step 2, if you like.

SERVES FOUR TO SIX

800g/1¾lb medium potatoes

100ml/3½fl oz/ scant ½ cup extra virgin olive oil

2 onions, thinly sliced

6 eggs

1 Thinly slice the potatoes. Heat 75ml/5 tbsp of the oil in a frying pan and cook the potatoes, turning frequently, for 10 minutes. Add the onions and seasoning, and continue to cook gently for a further 10 minutes, until the vegetables are tender.

2 Meanwhile, beat the eggs in a large bowl with a little seasoning. Add the potatoes and onions to the eggs and mix gently. Leave to stand for 10 minutes.

3 Wipe out the pan with kitchen paper and heat the remaining oil in it. Pour the egg mixture into the pan and spread it out in an even layer. Cover and cook over a very gentle heat for 20 minutes, until the eggs are just set. Serve cut into wedges.

Soups and Appetizers

All these fabulous first courses are simple to make, and many can be prepared in advance and just warmed before serving – leaving you free to enjoy the company of your guests.

Avocado Soup

This delicious soup has a fresh, delicate flavour and a wonderful colour. For added zest, add a generous squeeze of lime juice or spoon 15ml/1 tbsp salsa into the soup just before serving. Choose ripe avocados for this soup – they should feel soft when gently pressed. Keep very firm avocados at room temperature for 3–4 days until they soften. To speed ripening, place in a brown paper bag.

SERVES FOUR

2 large ripe avocados

300ml/½ pint/1¼ cups sour cream

1 litre/1¾ pints/ 4 cups well-flavoured chicken stock

small bunch of fresh coriander (cilantro)

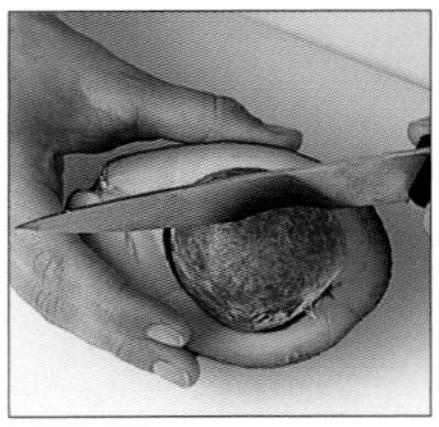

1 Cut the avocados in half, remove the peel and lift out the stones (pits). Chop the flesh coarsely and place it in a food processor with 45–60ml/3–4 tbsp of the sour cream. Process until smooth.

2 Heat the chicken stock in a pan. When it is hot, but still below simmering point, stir in the rest of the cream with salt to taste.

3 Gradually stir the avocado mixture into the hot stock. Heat gently but do not let the mixture approach boiling point.

4 Chop the coriander. Ladle the soup into individual heated bowls and sprinkle each portion with chopped coriander and black pepper. Serve immediately.

2 x 400g/14oz cans chopped tomatoes with herbs

250g/9oz cavolo nero leaves

400g/14oz can cannellini beans

60ml/4 tbsp extra virgin olive oil

Tuscan Bean Soup

Cavolo nero is a very dark green cabbage with a nutty flavour from Tuscany and southern Italy. It is ideal for this traditional recipe. It is available in most large supermarkets, but if you can't get it, use Savoy cabbage instead. Serve with ciabatta bread if you like.

SERVES FOUR

1 Pour the tomatoes into a large pan and add a can of cold water. Season with salt and pepper and bring to the boil, then reduce the heat to a simmer.

2 Roughly shred the cabbage leaves and add them to the pan. Partially cover the pan and simmer gently for about 15 minutes, or until the cabbage is tender.

3 Drain and rinse the cannellini beans, add to the pan and warm through for a few minutes. Check and adjust the seasoning, then ladle the soup into bowls, drizzle each one with a little olive oil and serve.

Winter Squash Soup with Tomato Salsa

Creamy butternut squash makes good soup with very few additional ingredients. Select a really good bought salsa for this soup and add a sprinkling of chopped fresh oregano or marjoram as a garnish.

SERVES FOUR TO FIVE

1 large butternut squash or small pumpkin, halved and seeded

75ml/5 tbsp garlic-flavoured olive oil

2 onions, chopped

60–120ml/4–8 tbsp tomato salsa

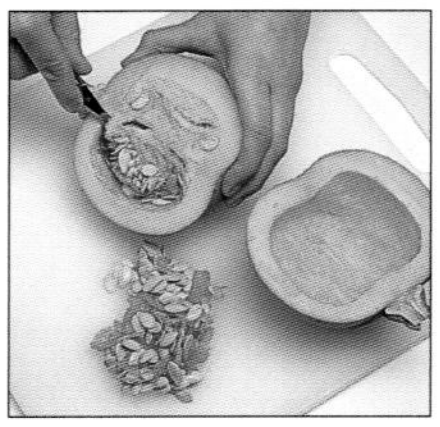

1 Preheat the oven to 220°C/425°F/Gas 7. Place the butternut squash or pumpkin on a baking sheet and brush with some of the oil and roast for 25 minutes. Reduce the temperature to 190°C/375°F/Gas 5 and cook for 20–25 minutes more, or until the squash is tender.

2 Heat the remaining oil in a large, heavy pan and cook the chopped onions over a low heat for about 10 minutes, or until softened.

3 Meanwhile, scoop the squash out of its skin, adding it to the pan. Pour in 1.2 litres/ 2 pints/5 cups water and stir in 5ml/1 tsp salt and plenty of black pepper. Bring to the boil, cover and simmer for 10 minutes.

4 Cool the soup slightly, then process it in a blender or food processor to a smooth purée. Alternatively, press the soup through a fine sieve with the back of a spoon. Reheat without boiling, then ladle it into warmed bowls. Top each serving with a spoonfuls of salsa and serve.

Stilton and Watercress Soup

A good creamy Stilton and plenty of peppery watercress bring maximum flavour to this rich, smooth soup, which is superlative in small portions. Rocket (arugula) can be used as an alternative to watercress – both leaves are an excellent source of iron. When choosing any salad leaves, look for crisp, fresh leaves and reject any wilted or discoloured greens.

SERVES FOUR TO SIX

1 Pour the stock into a pan and bring almost to the boil. Remove and discard any very large stalks from the watercress. Add the watercress to the pan and simmer gently for 2–3 minutes, until tender.

2 Crumble the cheese into the pan and simmer for 1 minute more, until the cheese has started to melt. Process the soup in a blender or food processor, in batches if necessary, until very smooth. Return the soup to the pan.

3 Stir in the cream and check the seasoning. The soup will probably not need any extra salt, as the blue cheese is already quite salty. Heat the soup gently, without boiling, then ladle it into warm bowls.

600ml/1 pint/ 2½ cups chicken or vegetable stock

225g/8oz watercress

150g/5oz Stilton or other blue cheese

150ml/¼ pint/⅔ cup single (light) cream

Curried Cauliflower Soup

This spicy, creamy soup is the perfect start to an elegant dinner party. You can also make broccoli soup in the same way, using the same weight of broccoli in place of the cauliflower. Serve with crusty bread and garnished with fresh coriander (cilantro) if you like.

SERVES FOUR

750ml/1¼ pints/3 cups milk

1 large cauliflower

15ml/1 tbsp garam masala

salt and ground black pepper

1 Pour the milk into a large pan and place over a medium heat. Cut the cauliflower into florets and add to the milk with the garam masala and season with salt and pepper.

2 Bring the milk to the boil, then reduce the heat, partially cover the pan with a lid and simmer for about 20 minutes, or until the cauliflower is tender.

3 Let the mixture cool for a few minutes, then transfer to a food processor and process until smooth (you may have to do this in two batches). Return the purée to the pan and heat through gently, checking and adjusting the seasoning, and serve immediately.

Pea Soup with Garlic

If you keep peas in the freezer, you can rustle up this delicious soup in minutes. It has a wonderfully sweet taste and smooth texture and is great served with crusty bread and garnished with mint.

SERVES FOUR

1 garlic clove, crushed

900g/2lb/8 cups frozen peas

1.2 litres/2 pints/5 cups chicken stock

25g/1oz/2 tbsp butter

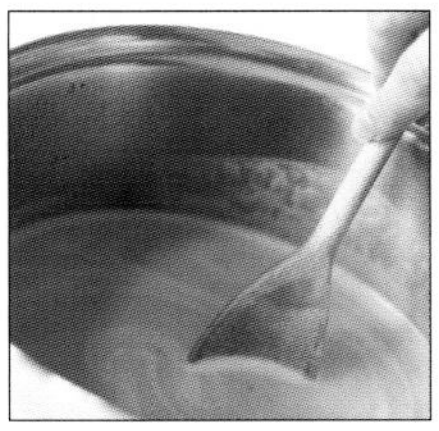

1 Heat the butter in a large pan and add the garlic. Fry gently for 2–3 minutes, until softened, then add the peas. Cook for 1–2 minutes more, then pour in the stock.

2 Bring the soup to the boil, then reduce the heat to a simmer. Cover the pan and cook for 5–6 minutes, until the peas are tender. Leave to cool slightly, then transfer the mixture to a food processor and process or until smooth (you may have to do this in two batches).

3 Return the soup to the pan and heat through gently. Season with salt and pepper.

Roast Asparagus with Crispy Prosciutto

Choose tender, fine asparagus for this recipe, as it cooks through quickly in the oven without losing its flavour or texture.

SERVES FOUR

350g/12oz fine asparagus spears, trimmed

1 small handful of fresh basil leaves

4 prosciutto slices

30ml/2 tbsp olive oil

1 Preheat the oven to 190°C/375°F/Gas 5. Put the asparagus in a roasting pan and drizzle with the olive oil. Sprinkle over the basil and season with salt and ground black pepper. Gently stir to coat in the oil, then spread the asparagus in a single layer.

2 Lay the slices of prosciutto on top of the asparagus and cook for 10–15 minutes, or until the prosciutto is crisp and the asparagus is just tender. Serve immediately.

Halloumi and Grape Salad

Firm and salty halloumi cheese is a great ingredient for turning a simple salad into a special dish. In this recipe it is tossed with sweet, juicy grapes, which complement its flavour and texture. Fresh young thyme leaves and dill taste especially good mixed with the salad.

SERVES FOUR

1 Toss together the salad leaves and fresh herb sprigs and the green and black grapes, then transfer to a large serving plate.

2 Thinly slice the halloumi cheese. Heat a large non-stick frying pan. Add the sliced halloumi cheese and cook briefly until it just starts to turn golden brown on the underside. Turn the cheese with a fish slice or metal spatula and cook the other side until it is golden brown.

3 Arrange the fried cheese over the salad on the plate. Pour over the oil and lemon juice or vinegar dressing and serve immediately while the cheese is still hot.

150g/5oz mixed salad leaves and tender fresh herb sprigs

175g/6oz mixed seedless green and black grapes

250g/9oz halloumi cheese

75ml/5 tbsp oil and lemon juice or vinegar dressing

Vegetarian, Fish and Shellfish

Roasted vegetables with cheese or a rich sauce make a substantial main course, and the delicate flavours of fish are beautifully captured in the simple, elegant dishes presented here.

Stuffed Baby Squash

It is worth making the most of baby squash while they are in season. Use any varieties you can find and do not worry too much about choosing vegetables of uniform size, as an assortment of different types and sizes looks attractive. The baked vegetables can easily be shared out at the table. Serve with warm sun-dried tomato bread and a ready-made spicy tomato sauce for a hearty vegetarian supper.

SERVES FOUR

4 small squash, each about 350g/12oz

200g/7oz/1 cup mixed wild and basmati rice

60ml/4 tbsp chilli and garlic oil

150g/5oz/1¼ cups grated Gruyère cheese

1 Preheat the oven to 190°C/375°F/Gas 5. Pierce the squash in several places with the tip of a knife. Bake for 30 minutes, until the squash are tender. Leave until cool enough to handle.

2 Meanwhile, cook the rice in salted, boiling water for 12 minutes, until tender, then drain. Slice a lid off the top of each squash and scoop out and discard the seeds. Scoop out and chop the flesh.

3 Heat the oil in a frying pan and cook the chopped squash for 5 minutes. Reserve 60ml/4 tbsp of the cheese, add the remainder to the pan with the rice and a little salt. Mix well.

4 Pile the mixture into the squash shells and place in an ovenproof dish. Sprinkle with the remaining cheese and bake for 20 minutes.

Aubergines with Cheese Sauce

This wonderfully simple dish of aubergines in cheese sauce is delicious hot and the perfect dish to assemble ahead of time ready for baking at the last minute. Kashkaval cheese is particularly good in this recipe – it is a hard yellow cheese made from sheep's milk and is originally from the Balkans. Serve with lots of crusty bread to mop up the delicious aubergine-flavoured cheese sauce.

SERVES FOUR TO SIX

2 large aubergines (eggplant), cut into 5mm/¼ in thick slices

about 60ml/4 tbsp olive oil

400g/14oz/3½ cups grated cheese, such as kashkaval, Gruyère, or a mixture of Parmesan and Cheddar

600ml/1 pint/2½ cups savoury white sauce or béchamel sauce

1 Layer the aubergine slices in a bowl or colander, sprinkling each layer with salt, and leave to drain for at least 30 minutes. Rinse well, then pat dry with kitchen paper.

2 Heat the oil in a frying pan, then cook the aubergine slices until golden brown on both sides. Remove from the pan and set aside.

3 Preheat the oven to 180°C/350°F/Gas 4. Mix most of the grated cheese into the savoury white or béchamel sauce, reserving a little to sprinkle on top of the finished dish.

4 Arrange a layer of the aubergines in an ovenproof dish, then pour over some sauce. Repeat, ending with sauce. Sprinkle with the reserved cheese. Bake for 35–40 minutes until golden.

Mushroom Polenta

This simple recipe uses freshly made polenta, but for an even easier version you can substitute ready-made polenta and slice it straight into the dish, ready for baking. The cheesy mushroom topping is also delicious on toasted herb or sun-dried tomato bread as a light lunch or supper. Any combination of mushrooms will work – try a mixture of button (white) and wild mushrooms as an alternative.

SERVES FOUR

250g/9oz/1½ cups quick-cook polenta

50g/2oz/ ¼ cup butter

400g/14oz chestnut mushrooms, sliced

175g/6oz/1½ cups grated Gruyère cheese

1 Line a 28 x 18cm/11 x 7in shallow baking tin (pan) with baking parchment. Bring 1 litre/1¾ pints/4 cups water with 5ml/1 tsp salt to the boil in a large pan. Add the polenta in a steady stream, stirring constantly. Bring back to the boil, stirring, and cook for 5 minutes, until thick and smooth. Turn the polenta into the prepared tin and spread it out into an even layer. Leave to cool.

2 Preheat the oven to 200°C/400°F/Gas 6. Melt the butter in a frying pan and cook the mushrooms for 3–5 minutes, until golden. Season with salt and lots of freshly ground black pepper.

3 Turn out the polenta on to a chopping board. Peel away the parchment and cut the polenta into large squares. Pile the squares into a shallow, ovenproof dish. Sprinkle with half the cheese, then pile the mushrooms on top and pour over their buttery juices. Sprinkle with the remaining cheese and bake for about 20 minutes, until the cheese is melting and pale golden.

Roasted Peppers with Halloumi and Pine Nuts

Halloumi cheese is creamy-tasting and has a firm texture and salty flavour that contrast well with the succulent sweet peppers. This is a good dish to assemble in advance. Halloumi is usually served cooked and lends itself well to barbecuing, frying or grilling (broiling). When heated the exterior hardens while the interior softens and is similar to mozzarella cheese.

SERVES FOUR

4 red and 2 orange or yellow (bell) peppers

60ml/4 tbsp garlic or herb olive oil

250g/9oz halloumi cheese

50g/2oz/½ cup pine nuts

1 Preheat the oven to 220°C/425°F/Gas 7. Halve the red peppers, leaving the stalks intact, and discard the seeds. Seed and coarsely chop the orange or yellow peppers. Place the red pepper halves on a baking sheet and fill with the chopped peppers. Drizzle with half the garlic or herb olive oil and bake for 25 minutes, until the edges of the peppers are beginning to char.

2 Dice the cheese and tuck in among the chopped peppers. Sprinkle with the pine nuts and drizzle with the remaining oil. Bake for a further 15 minutes, until well browned. Serve warm.

Roasted Aubergines with Feta and Coriander

Aubergines take on a lovely smoky flavour when grilled on a barbecue. Choose a good quality Greek feta cheese for the best flavour.

SERVES SIX

3 medium aubergines (eggplants)

400g/14oz feta cheese

a small bunch of coriander (cilantro), roughly chopped

60ml/4 tbsp extra virgin olive oil

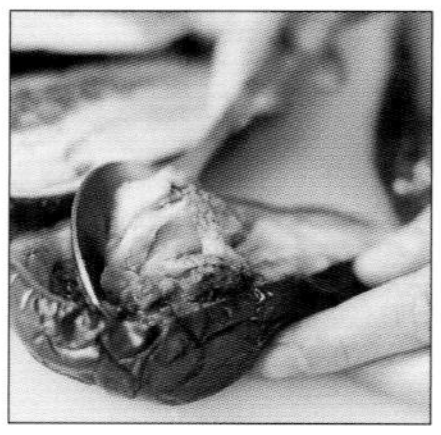

1 Prepare a barbecue. Cook the aubergines for 20 minutes, turning occasionally, until charred and soft. Remove from the barbecue and cut in half lengthways.

2 Carefully scoop the aubergine flesh into a bowl, reserving the skins. Mash the flesh roughly with a fork.

3 Crumble the feta cheese, then stir into the mashed aubergine with the chopped coriander and olive oil. Season with salt and ground black pepper to taste.

4 Spoon the aubergine and feta mixture back into the skins and return to the barbecue for 5 minutes to warm through. Serve immediately.

Pasta with Roast Tomatoes and Goat's Cheese

Roasting tomatoes brings out their flavour and sweetness, which contrasts perfectly with the sharp taste and creamy texture of goat's cheese. Serve with a crisp green salad flavoured with herbs.

SERVES FOUR

8 large ripe tomatoes

450g/1lb any dried pasta shapes

200g/7oz firm goat's cheese, crumbled

60ml/4 tbsp garlic-infused olive oil

1 Preheat the oven to 190°C/375°F/Gas 5. Place the tomatoes in a roasting pan and drizzle over 30ml/2 tbsp of the oil. Season well with salt and pepper and roast for 20–25 minutes, or until soft and slightly charred.

2 Meanwhile, cook the pasta in plenty of salted, boiling water, according to the instructions on the packet. Drain well and return to the pan.

3 Roughly mash the tomatoes with a fork, and stir the contents of the roasting pan into the pasta. Gently stir in the goat's cheese and the remaining oil and serve.

Crab Risotto

This simple risotto has a subtle flavour that makes the most of delicate crab and it makes a stylish main course. It is important to use a good quality risotto rice, which will give a deliciously creamy result, but the cooked grains are still firm to the bite.

SERVES THREE TO FOUR

2 large cooked crabs

275g/10oz/1½ cups risotto rice

1.2 litres/2 pints/ 5 cups simmering fish stock

30ml/2 tbsp mixed finely chopped fresh herbs such as chives, tarragon and parsley

1 One at a time, hold the crabs firmly and hit the underside with the heel of your hand. This should loosen the shell from the body. Using your thumbs, push against the body and pull away from the shell. Remove and discard the intestines and the grey gills.

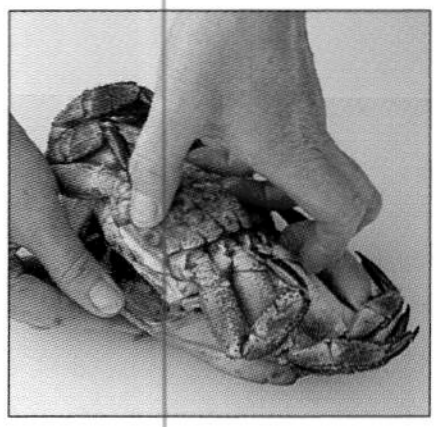

2 Break off the claws and legs, then use a hammer or crackers to break them open. Using a pick, remove the meat from the claws and legs. Place the meat on a plate.

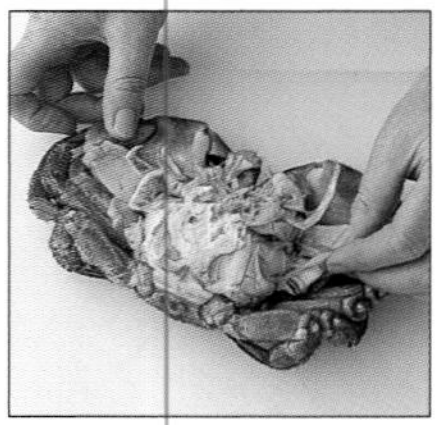

3 Using a skewer, pick out the white meat from the body cavities and place with the claw and leg meat, reserving a little white meat to garnish. Scoop out the brown meat from the shell and add to the rest of the crab meat.

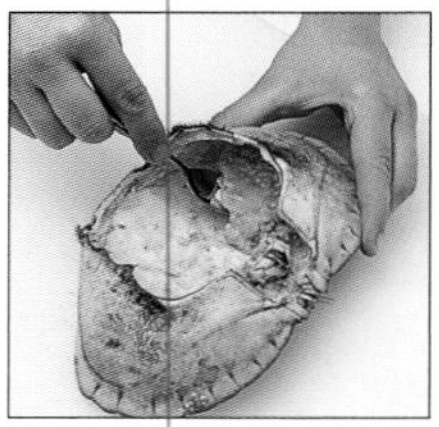

4 Place the rice in a pan and add one-quarter of the stock. Bring to the boil and cook, stirring, until the liquid has been absorbed. Adding a ladleful of stock at a time, cook, stirring, until about two-thirds of the stock has been absorbed. Stir in the crab meat and herbs, and continue cooking, adding the remaining stock.

5 When the rice is almost cooked but still has some bite, remove it from the heat and adjust the seasoning. Cover and leave to stand for 3 minutes. Serve garnished with the reserved white crab meat.

Filo-wrapped Fish

Select a chunky variety of tomato sauce for this simple but delicious recipe. The choice of fish can be varied according to what is in season and what is freshest on the day of purchase. When working with filo pastry, keep it covered with clear film (plastic wrap) or a damp dishtowel, as once it's exposed to air it dries out quickly and is difficult to handle.

SERVES THREE TO FOUR

about 130g/4½oz filo pastry (6–8 large sheets)

about 30ml/2 tbsp olive oil, for brushing

450g/1lb salmon or cod steaks or fillets

550ml/18fl oz/2½ cups fresh tomato sauce

1 Preheat the oven to 200°C/400°F/Gas 6. Take a sheet of filo pastry, brush with a little olive oil and cover with a second sheet of pastry. Place a piece of fish on top of the pastry, towards the bottom edge, then top with 1–2 spoonfuls of the tomato sauce, spreading it in an even layer.

2 Roll the fish in the pastry, taking care to enclose the filling completely. Brush with a little olive oil. Arrange on a baking sheet and repeat with the remaining fish and pastry. You should have about half the sauce remaining, to serve with the fish.

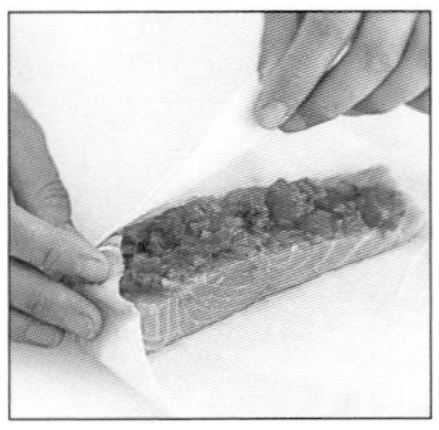

3 Bake for 10–15 minutes, or until golden. Meanwhile, reheat the remaining sauce. Serve immediately with the remaining sauce.

Haddock with Fennel Butter

Fresh fish tastes fabulous cooked in a simple herb butter. Here the liquorice flavour of fennel complements the haddock beautifully to make a simple dish ideal for a dinner party. If you can buy only small haddock fillets, fold them in half before baking, or use cod as an alternative. Serve tiny new potatoes and a herb salad with the fish to make a light, summery main course.

SERVES FOUR

675g/1½lb haddock fillet, skinned and cut into 4 portions

50g/2oz/¼ cup butter

1 lemon

45ml/3 tbsp coarsely chopped fennel

1 Preheat the oven to 220°C/425°F/Gas 7. Season the fish on both sides with salt and pepper. Melt one-quarter of the butter in a frying pan, preferably non-stick, and cook the fish over a medium heat briefly on both sides.

2 Transfer the fish to a shallow ovenproof dish. Cut four wafer-thin slices from the lemon and squeeze the juice from the remainder over the fish. Place the lemon slices on top and then bake for 15–20 minutes, or until the fish is cooked.

3 Meanwhile, melt the remaining butter in the frying pan and add the fennel and a little seasoning.

4 Transfer the cooked fish to plates and pour the cooking juices into the herb butter. Heat gently for a few seconds, then pour the herb butter over the fish. Serve immediately.

Roast Cod Wrapped in Prosciutto with Vine Tomatoes

Wrapping chunky fillets of cod in wafer-thin slices of prosciutto keeps the fish succulent and moist, at the same time adding flavour and visual impact. Serve with baby new potatoes and a herb salad for a stylish supper.

SERVES FOUR

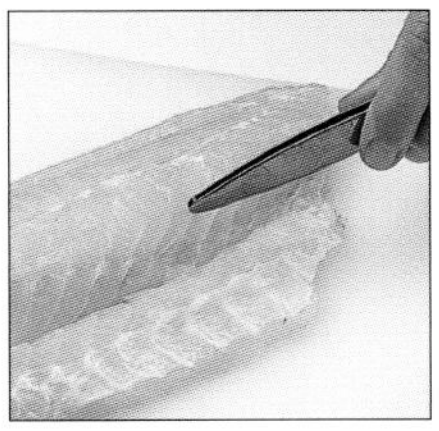

1 Preheat the oven to 220°C/425°F/Gas 7. Pat the fish dry on kitchen paper and remove any stray bones. Season lightly on both sides with salt and pepper.

2 Place one fillet in an ovenproof dish and drizzle 15ml/1 tbsp of the oil over it. Cover with the second fillet, laying the thick end on top of the thin end of the lower fillet to create an even shape. Lay the ham over the fish, overlapping the slices to cover the fish in an even layer. Tuck the ends of the ham under the fish and tie it in place at intervals with fine string.

3 Using kitchen scissors, snip the tomato vines into four portions and add to the dish. Drizzle the tomatoes and ham with the remaining oil and season lightly. Roast for about 35 minutes, until the tomatoes are tender and lightly coloured and the fish is cooked through. Test the fish by piercing one end of the parcel with the tip of a sharp knife to check that it flakes easily.

4 Slice the fish and transfer the portions to warm plates, adding the tomatoes. Spoon over the cooking juices from the dish and serve immediately.

2 thick skinless cod fillets, each weighing about 375g/13oz

75ml/5 tbsp extra virgin olive oil

75g/3oz prosciutto, thinly sliced

400g/14oz tomatoes, on the vine

Meat and Poultry

Your guests are sure to enjoy any one of the delicious dishes featured here – whether you choose homely, yet wonderfully flavoursome meatballs, or the impressive roast guinea fowl with luxurious whisky sauce.

Marinated Lamb with Oregano and Basil

Lamb leg steaks are chunky with a sweet flavour and go well with oregano and basil. However, you could also use finely chopped rosemary or thyme. Serve with couscous.

SERVES FOUR

4 large or 8 small lamb leg steaks

1 small bunch of fresh oregano, roughly chopped

1 small bunch of fresh basil, torn

60ml/4 tbsp garlic-infused olive oil

1 Put the lamb in a shallow, non-metallic dish. Mix 45ml/3 tbsp of the oil with the oregano, basil and some salt and pepper, reserving some of the herbs for garnish. Pour over the lamb and turn to coat in the marinade. Cover and chill for up to 8 hours.

2 Heat the remaining oil in a large frying pan. Remove the lamb from the marinade and fry for 5–6 minutes on each side, until slightly pink in the centre. Add the marinade and cook for 1–2 minutes until warmed through. Garnish with the reserved herbs and serve.

Beef Patties with Onions and Peppers

This is always popular. It is easy to make and delicious, and it can be varied by adding other vegetables, such as sliced red peppers, broccoli or mushrooms. These patties are very versatile and can be served in a variety of ways – with chunky home-made chips (fries), with crusty bread, or with rice and a ready-made tomato sauce.

SERVES FOUR

1 Place the minced beef, chopped onion and 15ml/1 tbsp garlic-flavoured oil in a bowl and mix well. Season well and form into four large or eight small patties.

2 Heat the remaining oil in a large non-stick pan, then add the patties and cook on both sides until browned. Sprinkle over 15ml/1 tbsp water and add a little seasoning.

3 Cover the patties with the sliced onions and peppers. Sprinkle in another 15ml/1 tbsp water and a little seasoning, then cover the pan. Reduce the heat to very low and braise for 20–30 minutes.

4 When the onions are turning golden brown, remove the pan from the heat. Serve the patties with onions and peppers.

500g/1¼lb lean minced (ground) beef

4 onions, 1 finely chopped and 3 sliced

30ml/2 tbsp garlic-flavoured olive oil or olive oil

2–3 green (bell) peppers, seeded and sliced lengthways into strips

Paprika Pork

This chunky, goulash-style dish is rich with peppers and paprika. Grilling the peppers before adding them to the meat really brings out their sweet, vibrant flavour. Rice or buttered boiled potatoes go particularly well with the rich pork.

SERVES FOUR

2 red, 1 yellow and 1 green (bell) pepper, seeded

500g/1¼lb lean pork fillet (tenderloin)

45ml/3 tbsp paprika

300g/11oz jar or tub of tomato sauce with herbs or garlic

1 Preheat the grill (broiler). Cut the peppers into thick strips and sprinkle in a single layer on a foil-lined grill rack. Cook under the grill for 20–25 minutes, until the edges of the strips are lightly charred.

2 Meanwhile, cut the pork into chunks. Season with salt and pepper and cook in a non-stick frying pan for about 5 minutes, until beginning to brown.

3 Transfer the meat to a heavy pan and add the paprika, tomato sauce, 300ml/½ pint/1¼ cups water and a little seasoning. Bring to the boil, reduce the heat, cover and simmer gently for 30 minutes.

4 Add the grilled (broiled) peppers and cook for a further 10–15 minutes, until the meat is tender. Taste for seasoning and serve immediately.

Soy-marinated Chicken

Two simple flavours, soy sauce and orange, combine to make this mouthwatering dish. Serving the chicken on a bed of asparagus turns the dish into a special treat. Wilted spinach or shredded greens work well as an everyday alternative. Boiled egg noodles or steamed white rice make a good accompaniment.

SERVES FOUR

4 skinless chicken breast fillets

1 large orange

30ml/2 tbsp dark soy sauce

400g/14oz medium asparagus spears

1 Slash each chicken portion diagonally and place them in a single layer in a shallow, ovenproof dish. Halve the orange, squeeze the juice from one half and mix it with the soy sauce. Pour this over the chicken. Cut the remaining orange into wedges and place these on the chicken. Cover and leave to marinate for several hours.

2 Preheat the oven to 180°C/350°F/Gas 4. Turn the chicken over and bake, uncovered, for 20 minutes. Turn the chicken over again and bake for a further 15 minutes, or until cooked through.

3 Meanwhile, cut off any tough ends from the asparagus and place in a frying pan. Pour in enough boiling water just to cover and cook gently for 3–4 minutes, until just tender. Drain and arrange on warmed plates, then top with the chicken and orange wedges. Spoon over the cooking juices and season with black pepper. Serve immediately.

Chicken Escalopes with Lemon and Serrano Ham

Chicken escalopes are flattened chicken breast fillets – they cook quicker than normal breast portions and absorb flavours more readily. In this light summery dish, the chicken absorbs the delicious flavours of the ham and lemon. It can be assembled in advance, so you can relax with your guests.

SERVES FOUR

40g/1½oz/3 tbsp butter, softened

4 skinless chicken breast fillets

4 slices Serrano ham

1 lemon

1 Preheat the oven to 180°C/350°F/Gas 4. Beat the butter with plenty of freshly ground black pepper and set aside. Place the chicken portions on a large sheet of clear film (plastic wrap), spacing them well apart. Cover with a second sheet, then beat with a rolling pin until the portions are half their original thickness.

2 Transfer the chicken to a large, shallow ovenproof dish and crumple a slice of ham on top of each. Cut eight thin slices from the lemon and place two on each slice of ham.

3 Dot with the pepper butter and bake for about 30 minutes, until the chicken is cooked. Transfer to serving plates and spoon over any juices from the dish.

Roast Chicken with Herb Cheese, Chilli and Lime Stuffing

This is a modern twist on the classic roast chicken – the stuffing is forced under the chicken skin, which helps to produce a wonderfully flavoured, succulent flesh. Serve the chicken with roast or mashed potatoes or rice, and a selection of steamed, seasonal vegetables.

SERVES FIVE TO SIX

1.8kg/4lb chicken

1 lime

115g/4oz/½ cup cream cheese with herbs and garlic

1 mild fresh red chilli, seeded and finely chopped

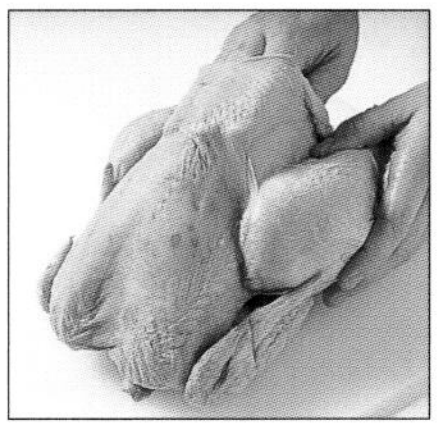

1 Preheat the oven to 200°C/400°F/Gas 6. Using first the point of a knife and then your fingers, separate the skin from the meat across the chicken breast and over the tops of the legs. Use the knife to loosen the first piece of skin, then carefully run your fingers underneath, taking care not to tear the skin.

2 Grate the lime and beat the rind into the cream cheese together with the chopped chilli. Pack the cream cheese stuffing under the skin, using a teaspoon, until fairly evenly distributed. Push the skin back into place, then smooth your hands over it to spread the stuffing in an even layer.

3 Put the chicken in a roasting pan and squeeze the juice from the lime over the top. Roast for 1½ hours, or until the juices run clear when the thickest part of the thigh is pierced with a skewer. If necessary, cover the chicken with foil towards the end of cooking if the top starts to become too browned.

4 Carve the chicken and arrange on a warmed serving platter. Spoon the pan juices over it and serve immediately.

Guinea Fowl with Whisky Sauce

Served with creamy, sweet mashed potato and lightly boiled whole baby leeks, guinea fowl is magnificent with a rich, creamy whisky sauce. If you don't like the flavour of whisky, then substitute brandy, Madeira or Marsala. Or, to make a non-alcoholic version, use freshly squeezed orange juice instead. Garnish with fresh thyme sprigs or other fresh herbs.

SERVES FOUR

2 guinea fowl, each weighing about 1kg/2¼lb

90ml/6 tbsp whisky

150ml/¼ pint/⅔ cup well-flavoured chicken stock

150ml/¼ pint/⅔ cup double (heavy) cream

1 Preheat the oven to 200°C/400°F/Gas 6. Brown the guinea fowl on all sides in a roasting pan on the hob (stovetop), then turn it breast uppermost and transfer the pan to the oven. Roast for about 1 hour, until the guinea fowl are golden and cooked through. Transfer the guinea fowl to a warmed serving dish, cover with foil and keep warm.

2 Pour off the excess fat from the pan, then heat the juices on the hob and stir in the whisky. Bring to the boil and cook until reduced. Add the stock and cream and simmer again until reduced slightly. Strain and season to taste.

3 Carve the guinea fowl and serve on individual plates, arranged around the chosen vegetable accompaniments. Sprinkle with plenty of freshly ground black pepper. Spoon a little of the sauce over each portion and serve the rest separately.

Duck with Plum Sauce

Sharp plums cut the rich flavour of duck wonderfully well in this updated version of an old English dish. Duck is often considered to be a fatty meat but modern breeding methods have made leaner ducks widely available. Good accompaniments to this dish would be creamy mashed potatoes and celeriac and steamed broccoli.

SERVES FOUR

4 duck quarters

1 large red onion, finely chopped

500g/1¼lb ripe plums, stoned (pitted) and quartered

30ml/2 tbsp redcurrant jelly

1 Prick the duck skin all over with a fork to release the fat during cooking and help give a crisp result, then place the portions in a heavy frying pan, skin side down.

2 Cook the duck pieces for 10 minutes on each side, or until golden brown and cooked right through. Remove the duck from the frying pan using a slotted spoon and keep warm.

3 Pour away all but 30ml/2 tbsp of the duck fat, then stir-fry the onion for 5 minutes, or until golden. Add the plums and cook for 5 minutes, stirring frequently. Add the jelly and mix well.

4 Replace the duck portions and cook for a further 5 minutes, or until thoroughly reheated. Season to taste before serving.

COOK'S TIP

It is important that the plums used in this dish are very ripe, otherwise the mixture will be too dry and the sauce will be extremely sharp.

Side Dishes and Salads

You can always accompany a main dish with simple steamed vegetables or fresh salad leaves, but for something extra special, try the recipes in this chapter – your guests are sure to be impressed.

Minty Broad Beans with Lemon

Young, tender broad beans have a sweet, mild taste and are delicious served in a simple salad. Take advantage of them when they're in season and make them into this fresh, zesty dish. Green peas – either fresh or frozen – are also delicious served in the same way, but you don't need to peel off their already tender skins.

SERVES FOUR

450g/1lb broad (fava) beans, thawed if frozen

grated rind and juice of 1 unwaxed lemon

1 small bunch of fresh mint, roughly chopped

30ml/2 tbsp garlic-infused olive oil

1 Using your fingers, slip the grey skins off the broad beans and discard – this takes a little time but the result is well worthwhile. Cook the beans in salted boiling water for 3–4 minutes, or until just tender.

2 Drain well and toss with the oil, lemon rind and juice, and mint. Season with salt and pepper, and serve immediately.

COOK'S TIP

When using fresh broad beans, it is easier to cook them first, then run them under cold water before slipping off their skins. Quickly blanch the skinned beans in boiling water to re-heat them.

Gingered Carrot Salad

This fresh and zesty salad is ideal served as an accompaniment to simple grilled chicken or fish. Some food processors have an attachment that can be used to cut the carrots into batons, which makes quick work of the preparation, but even cutting them by hand doesn't take too long. Fresh root ginger goes perfectly with sweet carrots, and the tiny black poppy seeds not only add taste and texture, but also look stunning against the bright orange of the carrots.

SERVES FOUR

350g/12oz carrots, peeled and cut into fine matchsticks

2.5cm/1in piece of fresh root ginger, peeled and grated

15ml/1 tbsp poppy seeds

30ml/2 tbsp garlic-infused olive oil

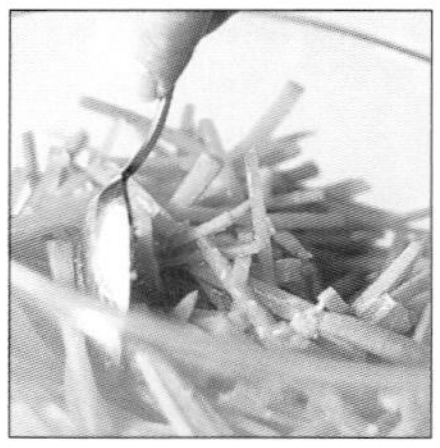

1 Put the carrots in a bowl and stir in the oil and grated ginger. Cover and chill for at least 30 minutes, to allow the flavours to develop.

2 Season the salad with salt and pepper to taste. Stir in the poppy seeds just before serving.

VARIATION

To make a parsnip and sesame seed salad, replace the carrots with parsnips and blanch in boiling salted water for 1 minute before combining with the oil and ginger. Replace the poppy seeds with the same quantity of sesame seeds.

Asparagus with Lemon Sauce

Sometimes less is more: here a simple egg and lemon dressing brings out the best in asparagus. When buying asparagus, look for bright coloured firm spears with tight buds – avoid those with tough woody stems. Choose roughly even-sized spears for uniform cooking.

SERVES FOUR

675g/1½lb asparagus, tough ends removed, and tied in a bundle

15ml/1 tbsp cornflour (cornstarch)

2 egg yolks

juice of 1½ lemons

1 Cook the bundle of asparagus in a tall pan of lightly salted, boiling water for 7–10 minutes.

2 Drain well and arrange the asparagus in a serving dish. Reserve 200ml/7fl oz/scant 1 cup of the cooking liquid.

3 Blend the cornflour with the cooled, reserved cooking liquid and place in a small pan. Bring to the boil, stirring constantly, and cook over a gentle heat until the sauce thickens slightly. Remove the pan from the heat and leave to cool slightly.

4 Beat the egg yolks thoroughly with the lemon juice and gradually stir into the cooled sauce. Cook over a very low heat, stirring constantly, until the sauce is fairly thick. Be careful not to overheat the sauce or it may curdle. As soon as the sauce has thickened, remove the pan from the heat and continue stirring for 1 minute. Taste and season with salt. Leave the sauce to cool slightly.

5 Stir the cooled lemon sauce, then pour a little over the cooked asparagus. Cover and chill in the refrigerator for at least 2 hours before serving with the rest of the sauce to accompany.

COOK'S TIP

For a slightly less tangy sauce, add a little caster (superfine) sugar with the salt in step 4.

Braised Lettuce and Peas with Spring Onions

This light vegetable dish is based on the classic French method of braising peas with lettuce and spring onions in butter, and is delicious served with simply grilled fish or roast or grilled duck. A sprinkling of chopped fresh mint makes a fresh, flavoursome and extremely pretty garnish. Other legumes such as broad (fava) beans, mangetouts (snow peas) and sugar snaps can be used instead of peas to create a delicious variation.

SERVES FOUR

50g/2oz/¼ cup butter

4 Little Gem (Bibb) lettuces, halved lengthways

2 bunches spring onions (scallions), trimmed

400g/14oz shelled peas (about 1kg/2¼lb in pods)

1 Melt half the butter in a wide, heavy pan over a low heat. Add the lettuces and spring onions.

2 Turn the vegetables in the butter, then sprinkle in salt and plenty of freshly ground black pepper. Cover, and cook the vegetables very gently for 5 minutes, stirring once.

3 Add the peas and turn them in the buttery juices. Pour in 120ml/4fl oz/½ cup water, then cover and cook over a gentle heat for a further 5 minutes. Uncover and increase the heat to reduce the liquid to a few tablespoons.

4 Stir in the remaining butter and adjust the seasoning. Transfer to a warmed serving dish and serve immediately.

EXTRAS

- *Braise about 250g/9oz baby carrots with the lettuce.*
- *Cook 115g/4oz chopped smoked bacon or pancetta in the butter. Use one bunch of spring onions (scallions) and stir in some chopped parsley.*

Champ

This traditional Irish dish of potatoes and green or spring onions is enriched with a wickedly indulgent amount of butter – for even more decadence, replace 60ml/4 tbsp of the milk with crème fraîche or buttermilk.

SERVES FOUR

1kg/2¼ lb potatoes, cut into chunks

300ml/½ pint/1¼ cups milk

1 bunch spring onions (scallions), thinly sliced, plus extra to garnish

115g/4oz/½ cup slightly salted butter

1 Boil the potatoes in lightly salted water for 20–25 minutes, or until they are tender. Drain and mash the potatoes with a fork until smooth.

2 Place the milk, spring onions and half the butter in a small pan and set over a low heat until just simmering. Cook for 2–3 minutes, until the butter has melted and the spring onions have softened.

3 Beat the milk mixture into the mashed potato using a wooden spoon until the mixture is light and fluffy. Reheat gently, adding seasoning to taste.

4 Turn the potato into a warmed serving dish and make a well in the centre with a spoon. Place the remaining butter in the well and let it melt. Serve immediately, sprinkled with extra spring onion.

EXTRAS

To make colcannon, another Irish speciality, follow the main recipe, using half the butter. Cook about 500g/1¼ lb finely shredded green cabbage or kale in a little water until just tender, drain thoroughly and then beat into the creamed potato. This is delicious served with sausages and grilled (broiled) ham or bacon. The colcannon may also be fried in butter and then browned under the grill (broiler).

Asparagus, Bacon and Leaf Salad

This excellent salad turns a plain roast chicken or simple grilled fish into an interesting meal, especially when served with buttered new potatoes. A wide range of different salad leaves are readily available – frisée has feathery, curly, slightly bitter tasting leaves and is a member of the chicory family. Frisée leaves range in colour from yellow-white to yellow-green.

SERVES FOUR

500g/1¼lb medium asparagus spears

130g/4½oz thin-cut smoked back (lean) bacon

250g/9oz frisée lettuce leaves or mixed leaf salad

100ml/3½fl oz/ scant ½ cup French dressing

1 Trim off any tough stalk ends from the asparagus and cut the spears into three, setting the tender tips aside. Heat a 1cm/½in depth of water in a frying pan until simmering. Reserve the asparagus tips and cook the remainder of the spears in the water for about 3 minutes, until almost tender. Add the tips and cook for 1 minute more. Drain and refresh under cold, running water.

2 Dry-fry the bacon until golden and crisp and then set it aside to cool slightly. Use kitchen scissors to snip it into bitesize pieces. Place the frisée or mixed leaf salad in a bowl and add the bacon.

3 Add the asparagus and a little black pepper to the salad. Pour the dressing over and toss the salad lightly, then serve before the leaves begin to wilt.

Warm Chorizo and Spinach Salad

Spanish chorizo sausage contributes an intense spiciness to any ingredient with which it is cooked. In this hearty warm salad, spinach has sufficient flavour to compete with the chorizo. Watercress or rocket (arugula) could be used instead of the spinach, if you prefer. For an added dimension use a flavoured olive oil – rosemary, garlic or chilli oil would work perfectly. Serve the salad with warm crusty bread to soak up all the delicious cooking juices.

SERVES FOUR

225g/8oz baby spinach leaves

90ml/6 tbsp extra virgin olive oil

150g/5oz chorizo sausage, very thinly sliced

30ml/2 tbsp sherry vinegar

1 Discard any tough stalks from the spinach. Pour the oil into a large frying pan and add the sausage. Cook gently for 3 minutes, until the sausage slices start to shrivel slightly and colour.

2 Add the spinach leaves and remove the pan from the heat. Toss the spinach in the warm oil until it just starts to wilt. Add the sherry vinegar and a little seasoning. Toss the ingredients briefly, then serve immediately, while still warm.

Potato and Olive Salad

This delicious salad is simple and zesty – try it with a vegetarian main dish such as roasted peppers or other vegetables, or even with roast chicken. Fresh coriander is similar in appearance to flat leaf parsley, but has a distinctive pungent, almost spicy flavour. It is widely used in India, the Middle and Far East and in eastern Mediterranean countries.

SERVES FOUR

8 large new potatoes

45–60ml/3–4 tbsp garlic-flavoured oil and vinegar dressing

60–90ml/4–6 tbsp chopped fresh herbs, such as coriander (cilantro) and chives

10–15 dry-fleshed black Mediterranean olives

1 Cut the new potatoes into chunks. Put them in a pan, pour in water to cover and add a pinch of salt. Bring to the boil, then reduce the heat and cook gently for about 10 minutes, or until the potatoes are just tender. Drain well and leave in a colander to dry thoroughly and cool slightly.

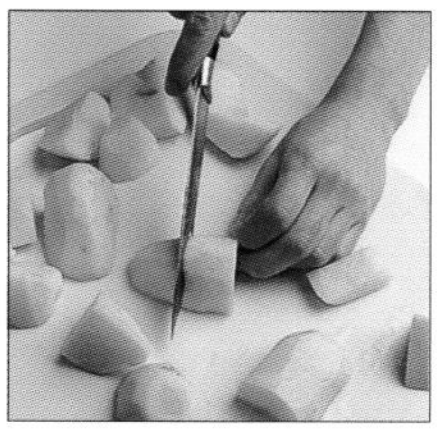

2 When they are cool enough to handle, chop the potatoes and put them in a serving bowl.

3 Drizzle the garlic dressing over the potatoes. Toss well and sprinkle with the chopped fresh coriander and chives, and black olives. Chill in the refrigerator for at least 1 hour before serving.

EXTRAS *Add a sprinkling of paprika and roasted whole cumin seeds to spice up the salad.*

Hot Desserts

A hot dessert makes the perfect end to a dinner and can take very little time to prepare. Many of the recipes in this chapter can be made in advance and simply popped in the oven, freeing up your time for entertaining.

Grilled Peaches with Meringues

Ripe peaches take on a fabulous scented fruitiness when grilled with brown sugar, and mini meringues are the perfect accompaniment. Serve with crème fraîche flavoured with a little grated orange rind. When buying peaches or nectarines, choose fruit with an attractive rosy bloom, avoiding any that have a green-tinged skin or feel hard. Nectarines have a smoother skin than peaches and are actually a type of peach native to China.

SERVES SIX

2 egg whites

115g/4oz/½ cup soft light brown sugar, reserving 5ml/1 tsp for the peaches

pinch of ground cinnamon

6 ripe peaches, or nectarines

1 Preheat the oven to 140°C/275°F/Gas 1. Line two large baking sheets with baking parchment.

2 Whisk the egg whites until they form stiff peaks. Gradually whisk in the sugar and ground cinnamon until the mixture is stiff and glossy. Pipe 18 very small meringues on to the trays and bake for 40 minutes. Leave in the oven to cool.

3 Meanwhile, halve and stone (pit) the peaches or nectarines, sprinkling each half with a little sugar as it is cut. Grill (broil) for 4–5 minutes, until just beginning to caramelize.

4 Arrange the grilled peaches on serving plates with the meringues and serve immediately.

COOK'S TIP

Use leftover egg whites to make these little cinnamon-flavoured meringues. The meringues can be stored in an airtight container for about 2 weeks. Serve them after dinner with coffee or with desserts.

Apricot and Ginger Gratin

Made with tangy fresh apricots, this quick and easy dessert has a comforting, baked cheesecake-like flavour. For an even easier version of this delicious gratin, use 400g/14oz canned apricots in juice. Use juice from the can to beat into the cream cheese.

SERVES FOUR

1 Put the apricots in a pan with the sugar. Pour in 75ml/5 tbsp water and heat until barely simmering. Cover and cook very gently for 8–10 minutes, until they are tender but still holding their shape.

2 Preheat the oven to 200°C/400°F/Gas 6. Drain the apricots, reserving the syrup, and place in a large dish or divide among four individual ovenproof dishes. Set aside 90ml/6 tbsp of the syrup and spoon the remainder over the fruit.

3 Beat the cream cheese until softened, then gradually beat in the reserved syrup until smooth. Spoon the cheese mixture over the apricots. Sprinkle the biscuit crumbs over the cream cheese and juice mixture. Bake for 10 minutes, until the crumb topping is beginning to darken and the filling has warmed through. Serve immediately.

500g/1¼ lb apricots, halved and stoned (pitted)

75g/3oz/scant ½ cup caster (superfine) sugar

200g/7oz/scant 1 cup cream cheese

75g/3oz gingernut biscuits (gingersnaps), crushed to crumbs

Baked Ricotta Cakes with Red Sauce

These honey-flavoured desserts take only minutes to make from a few ingredients. The fragrant fruity sauce provides a contrast of both colour and flavour. The red berry sauce can be made a day in advance and chilled until ready to use. Frozen fruit doesn't need extra water, as it usually yields its juice easily on thawing.

SERVES FOUR

250g/9oz/generous 1 cup ricotta cheese

2 egg whites, beaten

60ml/4 tbsp scented honey, plus extra to taste

450g/1lb/4 cups mixed fresh or frozen fruit, such as strawberries, raspberries, blackberries and cherries

1 Preheat the oven to 180°C/350°F/Gas 4. Place the ricotta cheese in a bowl and break it up with a wooden spoon. Add the beaten egg whites and honey, and mix thoroughly until smooth and well combined.

2 Lightly grease four ramekins. Spoon the ricotta mixture into the prepared ramekins and level the tops. Bake for 20 minutes, or until the ricotta cakes are risen and golden.

3 Meanwhile, make the fruit sauce. Reserve about one-quarter of the fruit for decoration. Place the rest of the fruit in a pan, with a little water if the fruit is fresh, and heat gently until softened. Leave to cool slightly and remove any stones (pits) if using cherries.

4 Press the fruit through a sieve (strainer), then taste and sweeten with honey if it is too tart. Serve the sauce, warm or cold, with the ricotta cakes. Decorate with the reserved berries.

Hot Blackberry and Apple Soufflé

The deliciously tart flavours of blackberry and apple complement each other perfectly to make a light, mouthwatering and surprisingly low-fat, hot dessert. Running a table knife around the inside edge of the soufflé dishes before baking helps the soufflés to rise evenly without sticking to the rim of the dish. Make this dish in early autumn, when there are plentiful supplies of blackberries.

MAKES SIX

350g/12oz/3 cups blackberries

1 large cooking apple, peeled and finely diced

3 egg whites

150g/5oz/¾ cup caster (superfine) sugar, plus extra caster or icing (confectioners') sugar for dusting

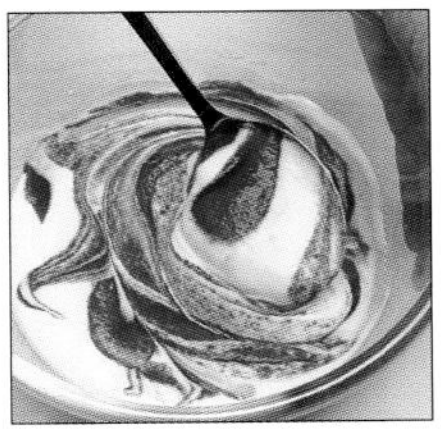

1 Preheat the oven to 200°C/400°F/Gas 6. Put a baking sheet in the oven to heat. Cook the blackberries and apple in a pan for 10 minutes, or until the juice runs from the blackberries and the apple has pulped down well. Press through a sieve into a bowl. Stir in 50g/2oz/¼ cup caster sugar. Set aside to cool.

2 Put a spoonful of the fruit purée into each of six 150ml/¼ pint/⅔ cup greased and sugared individual soufflé dishes and smooth the surface. Set the dishes aside.

3 Whisk the egg whites in a large bowl until they form stiff peaks. Gradually whisk in the remaining caster sugar. Fold in the remaining fruit purée and spoon the flavoured meringue into the prepared dishes. Level the tops with a palette knife (metal spatula) and run a table knife around the edge of each dish.

4 Place the dishes on the hot baking sheet and bake for 10–15 minutes, until the soufflés have risen well and are lightly browned. Dust the tops with a little sugar and serve immediately.

Treacle Tart

The best chilled commercial shortcrust pastry makes light work of this old-fashioned favourite, with its sticky filling and twisted lattice topping. Smooth creamy custard is the classic accompaniment, but it is also delicious served with cream or ice cream. For a more textured filling, use wholemeal (whole-wheat) breadcrumbs or crushed cornflakes instead of the white breadcrumbs.

SERVES FOUR TO SIX

350g/12oz shortcrust pastry

260g/9½oz/generous ¾ cup golden (light corn) syrup

1 lemon

75g/3oz/1½ cups fresh white breadcrumbs

1 On a lightly floured surface, roll out three-quarters of the pastry to a thickness of 3mm/⅛in. Transfer to a 20cm/8in fluted flan tin (pan) and trim off the overhang. Chill the pastry case (pie shell) for 20 minutes. Reserve the pastry trimmings.

2 Put a baking sheet in the oven and preheat to 200°C/400°F/Gas 6. To make the filling, warm the syrup in a pan until it melts. Grate the lemon rind and squeeze the juice.

3 Remove the syrup from the heat and stir in the breadcrumbs and lemon rind. Leave to stand for 10 minutes, then add more crumbs if the mixture is too thin and moist. Stir in 30ml/2 tbsp of the lemon juice, then spread the mixture evenly in the pastry case.

4 Roll out the reserved pastry and cut into 10–12 thin strips. Twist the strips into spirals, then lay half of them on the filling. Arrange the remaining strips at right angles to form a lattice. Press the ends on to the rim.

5 Place the tart on the hot baking sheet and bake for 10 minutes. Lower the oven temperature to 190°C/375°F/Gas 5. Bake for 15 minutes more, until golden. Serve warm.

Hot Chocolate Rum Soufflés

Light as air, melt-in-the-mouth soufflés are always impressive, yet they are often based on the simplest store-cupboard ingredients. Serve them as soon as they are cooked for a fantastic finale to a special dinner party. For an extra indulgent touch, serve the soufflés with whipped cream flavoured with dark rum and grated orange rind.

SERVES SIX

50g/2oz/½ cup unsweetened cocoa powder

65g/2½oz/5 tbsp caster (superfine) sugar, plus extra caster or icing (confectioners') sugar for dusting

30ml/2 tbsp dark rum

6 egg whites

COOK'S TIP *When serving the soufflés at the end of a dinner party, prepare them just before the meal is served. Put them in the oven when the main course is finished and serve steaming hot.*

1 Preheat the oven to 190°C/375°F/Gas 3. Place a baking sheet in the oven to heat up.

2 Mix 15ml/1 tbsp of the cocoa with 15ml/1 tbsp of the sugar in a bowl. Grease six 250ml/8fl oz/1 cup ramekins. Pour the cocoa and sugar mixture into each of the dishes in turn, rotating them so that they are evenly coated.

3 Mix the remaining cocoa powder with the dark rum.

4 Whisk the egg whites in a clean, grease-free bowl until they form stiff peaks. Whisk in the remaining sugar. Stir a generous spoonful of the whites into the cocoa mixture to lighten it, then fold in the remaining whites.

5 Divide the mixture among the dishes. Place on the hot baking sheet, and bake for 13–15 minutes, or until well risen. Dust with caster or icing sugar before serving.

Caramelized Upside-down Pear Pie

In this gloriously sticky dessert, which is almost like the French classic *tarte tatin*, the pastry is baked on top of the fruit, which gives it a crisp and flaky texture. When inverted, the pie looks wonderful. Look for good-quality chilled pastry that you can freeze for future use. Serve with whipped cream, ice cream or just plain for a gloriously sticky dessert.

SERVES EIGHT

5–6 firm, ripe pears

175g/6oz/scant 1 cup caster (superfine) sugar

115g/4oz/½ cup butter

225g/8oz unsweetened shortcrust pastry

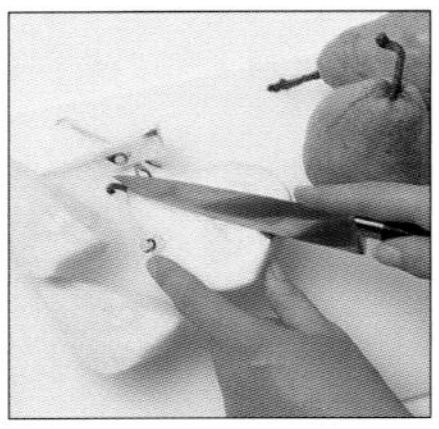

1 Peel, quarter and core the pears. Toss with some of the sugar in a bowl.

2 Melt the butter in a 27cm/10½in heavy, ovenproof omelette pan. Add the remaining sugar. When it changes colour, arrange the pears in the pan.

3 Continue cooking, uncovered, for 20 minutes, or until the fruit has completely caramelized.

4 Leave the fruit to cool in the pan. Preheat the oven to 200°C/400°F/Gas 6. Meanwhile, on a lightly floured surface, roll out the pastry to a round that is slightly larger than the diameter of the pan. Lay the pastry on top of the pears and then carefully tuck it in around the edge.

5 Bake for 15 minutes, then lower the oven temperature to 180°C/350°F/Gas 4. Bake for a further 15 minutes, or until the pastry is golden.

6 Let the pie cool in the pan for a few minutes. To unmould, run a knife around the pan's edge, then, using oven gloves, invert a plate over the pan and quickly turn the two over together.

7 If any pears stick to the pan, remove them gently with a palette knife (metal spatula) and replace them on the pie. The pie is best served warm.

VARIATIONS

• *To make caramelized upside-down apple pie, replace the pears with eight or nine firm, full-flavoured eating apples – Cox's Orange Pippins would be a good choice. You will need more apples than pears, as they shrink during cooking.*

• *Nectarines or peaches also work well, as does rhubarb. Rhubarb is tart, so you may need to add more sugar.*

Blueberry and Almond Tart

This is a cheat's version of a sweet almond tart and the result is superb. Whisked egg whites and grated marzipan cook to form a light sponge under a tangy topping of contrasting blueberries. When whisking the egg whites for the filling, ensure all traces of yolk are removed – otherwise you won't be able to whisk them to their maximum volume.

SERVES SIX

250g/9oz shortcrust pastry

175g/6oz/generous 1 cup white marzipan

4 large (US extra large) egg whites

130g/4½oz/ generous 1 cup blueberries

1 Preheat the oven to 200°C/400°F/Gas 6. Roll out the pastry and use to line a 23cm/9in round, loose-based flan tin (pan). Line with greaseproof (waxed) paper and fill with baking beans, then bake for 15 minutes. Remove the beans and greaseproof paper and bake for a further 5 minutes. Reduce the oven temperature to 180°C/350°F/Gas 4.

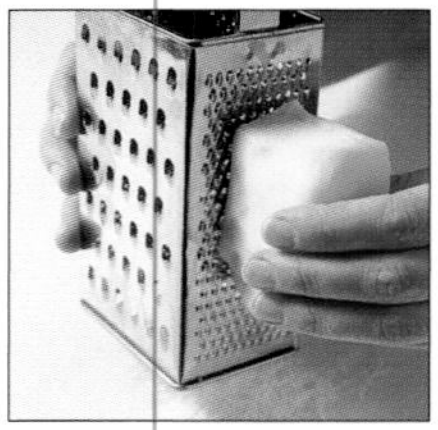

2 Grate the marzipan. Whisk the egg whites until stiff. Sprinkle half the marzipan over them and fold in. Then fold in the rest.

3 Turn the mixture into the pastry case (pie shell) and spread it evenly. Sprinkle the blueberries over the top and bake for 20–25 minutes, until golden and just set. Leave to cool for 10 minutes before serving.

Baked Bananas with Ice Cream and Toffee Sauce

Bananas make one of the easiest of all desserts, just as welcome as a comforting winter treat as they are to follow a barbecue. For an extra sweet finishing touch, grate some plain (semisweet) chocolate on the bananas, over the sauce, just before serving. If baking on a barbecue, turn the bananas occasionally to ensure even cooking.

SERVES FOUR

4 large bananas

75g/3oz/scant ½ cup light muscovado (brown) sugar

75ml/5 tbsp double (heavy) cream

4 scoops good-quality vanilla ice cream

1 Preheat the oven to 180°C/350°F/Gas 4. Put the unpeeled bananas in an ovenproof dish and bake for 15–20 minutes, until the skins are very dark and the flesh feels soft when squeezed.

2 Meanwhile, heat the light muscovado sugar in a small, heavy pan with 75ml/5 tbsp water until dissolved. Bring to the boil and add the double cream. Cook for 5 minutes, until the sauce has thickened and is toffee coloured. Remove from the heat.

3 Transfer the baked bananas in their skins to serving plates and split them lengthways to reveal the flesh. Pour some of the sauce over the bananas and top with scoops of vanilla ice cream. Serve any remaining sauce separately.

Ice Creams and Cold Desserts

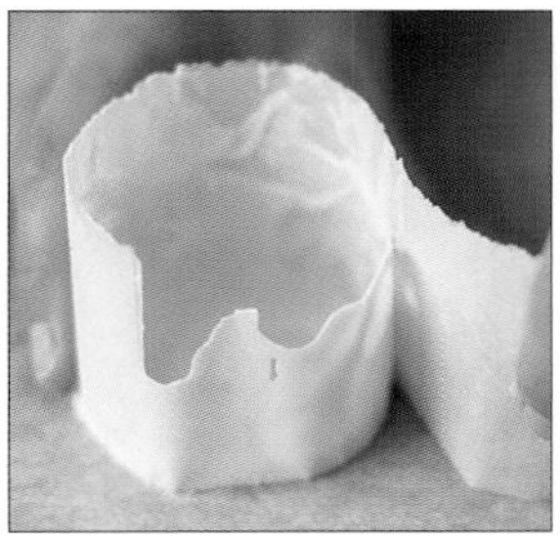

Because they can be made in advance, ice creams and cold desserts are the perfect choice for entertaining. All the recipes in this chapter have an elegant simplicity that will guarantee success with even the most sophisticated dinner guests.

Lemon Sorbet

This is probably the most classic sorbet of all. Refreshingly tangy and yet deliciously smooth, it quite literally melts in the mouth. Try to buy unwaxed lemons for recipes such as this one where the lemon rind is used. The wax coating can adversely affect the flavour of the rind.

SERVES SIX

200g/7oz/1 cup caster (superfine) sugar, plus extra for coating rind to decorate

4 lemons, well scrubbed

1 egg white

1 Put the sugar in a pan and pour in 300ml/½ pint/1¼ cups water. Bring to the boil, stirring occasionally until the sugar has just dissolved.

2 Using a swivel vegetable peeler, pare the rind thinly from two of the lemons so that it falls straight into the pan.

3 Simmer for 2 minutes without stirring, then take the pan off the heat. Leave to cool, then chill.

4 Squeeze the juice from all the lemons and add it to the syrup. Strain the syrup into a shallow freezerproof container, reserving the rind. Freeze the mixture for 4 hours, until it is mushy.

5 Process the sorbet in a food processor until it is smooth. Lightly whisk the egg white with a fork until it is just frothy. Replace the sorbet in the container, beat in the egg white and return the mixture to the freezer for 4 hours, or until it is firm.

6 Cut the reserved lemon rind into fine shreds and cook them in boiling water for 5 minutes, or until tender. Drain, then place on a plate and sprinkle generously with caster sugar. Scoop the sorbet into bowls or glasses and decorate with the sugared lemon rind.

Strawberry and Lavender Sorbet

A hint of lavender transforms a familiar strawberry sorbet into a perfumed dinner-party dessert. When buying strawberries look for plump, shiny fruit without any signs of straining or leakage at the bottom of the punnet – this suggests that the fruit at the bottom has been squashed. To hull strawberries, prise out the leafy top with a sharp knife or a specially designed strawberry huller.

SERVES SIX

150g/5oz/¾ cup caster (superfine) sugar

6 fresh lavender flowers, plus extra to decorate

500g/1¼lb/5 cups strawberries, hulled

1 egg white

1 Place the sugar in a pan and pour in 300ml/½ pint/1¼ cups water. Bring to the boil, stirring until the sugar has dissolved.

2 Take the pan off the heat, add the lavender flowers and leave to infuse (steep) for 1 hour. If time permits, chill the syrup in the refrigerator before using.

3 Process the strawberries in a food processor or in batches in a blender, then press the purée through a large sieve into a bowl.

4 Pour the purée into a freezerproof container, strain in the syrup and freeze for 4 hours, or until mushy. Transfer to a food processor and process until smooth. Whisk the egg white until frothy, and stir into the sorbet. Spoon the sorbet back into the container and freeze until firm.

5 Serve in scoops, piled into tall glasses, and decorate with sprigs of lavender flowers.

COOK'S TIP

The size of the lavender flowers can vary; if they are very small, you may need to use eight. To double check, taste a little of the cooled lavender syrup. If you think the flavour is too mild, add two or three more flowers, reheat and cool again before using.

Kulfi

This favourite Indian ice cream is traditionally made by carefully boiling milk until it has reduced to about one-third of its original quantity. Although you can save time by using condensed milk, nothing beats the luscious result achieved by using the authentic method. When they are available, rose petals are a stylish decoration in addition to the pistachio nuts.

SERVES FOUR

1.5 litres/2½ pints/6¼ cups full-fat (whole) milk

3 cardamom pods

25g/1oz/2 tbsp caster (superfine) sugar

50g/2oz/½ cup pistachio nuts, skinned

1 Pour the milk into a large, heavy pan. Bring to the boil, reduce the heat and simmer gently for 1 hour, stirring occasionally.

2 Put the cardamom pods in a mortar and crush them with a pestle. Add the pods and the seeds to the milk and continue to simmer, stirring frequently, for 1–1½ hours, or until the milk has reduced to about 475ml/16fl oz/2 cups. Strain the milk into a jug (pitcher), stir in the sugar and leave to cool.

3 Grind half the pistachios in a blender or nut grinder. Cut the remaining pistachios into thin slivers and set them aside for decoration. Stir the ground nuts into the milk mixture.

4 Pour the milk and pistachio mixture into four kulfi or lolly (popsicle) moulds. Freeze the mixture overnight or until firm.

5 To unmould the kulfi, half fill a plastic container or bowl with very hot water, stand the moulds in the water and count to ten. Immediately lift out the moulds and invert them on a baking sheet. Transfer the ice creams to individual plates and sprinkle sliced pistachios over the top.

Caramel and Pecan Terrine

Frozen or long-life cream is a useful ingredient for making impressive desserts without having a mega shopping trip. Caramel and nuts transform cream to parfait in this recipe. Take care that the syrup does not become too dark, or the ice cream will taste bitter.

SERVES SIX

115g/4oz/generous ½ cup sugar

450ml/¾ pint/scant 2 cups double (heavy) cream

30ml/2 tbsp icing (confectioners') sugar

75g/3oz/¾ cup pecan nuts, toasted

COOK'S TIP

Watch the caramel syrup closely after removing it from the heat. If it starts to turn too dark, dip the base of the pan in cold water. If the syrup remains very pale, return the pan to the heat and cook it for a little longer.

1 Heat the sugar and 75ml/5 tbsp water in a small, heavy pan until the sugar dissolves. Boil rapidly until the sugar has turned pale golden. Remove the pan from the heat and leave to stand until the syrup turns a rich brown colour.

2 Pour 90ml/6 tbsp of the cream over the caramel. Heat to make a smooth sauce. Leave to cool.

3 Rinse a 450g/1lb loaf tin (pan), then line the base and sides with clear film (plastic wrap). Whip a further 150ml/¼ pint/⅔cup of the cream with the icing sugar until it forms soft peaks. Whip the remaining cream separately and stir in the caramel sauce and the toasted pecan nuts.

4 Spoon one-third of the caramel cream into the prepared tin and spread with half the plain whipped cream. Spread half of the remaining caramel cream over the top, then top with the last of the plain cream. Finally, add the remaining caramel cream and level the surface. Freeze for 6 hours.

5 To serve, dip the tin in very hot water for 2 seconds, invert it on to a serving plate and peel away the film. Serve sliced.

Baked Custard with Burnt Sugar

This delicious egg custard or crème brûlée is a rich indulgent dessert that can be prepared well in advance. You can buy vanilla sugar or make your own by placing a split vanilla pod (bean) in a jar of caster (superfine) sugar – the sugar will be ready to use after a couple of days.

SERVES SIX

1 litre/1¾ pints/4 cups double (heavy) cream

6 egg yolks

90g/3½oz/½ cup vanilla sugar

75g/3oz/⅓ cup soft light brown sugar

1 Preheat the oven to 150°C/300°F/Gas 2. Place six 120ml/ 4fl oz/½ cup ramekins in a roasting pan or ovenproof dish and set aside while you prepare the vanilla custard.

2 Heat the double cream in a heavy pan over a gentle heat until it is very hot, but not boiling.

3 In a bowl, whisk the egg yolks and vanilla sugar until well blended. Whisk in the hot cream and strain into a large jug (pitcher). Divide the custard equally among the ramekins.

4 Pour enough boiling water into the roasting pan to come about halfway up the sides of the ramekins. Cover the pan with foil and bake for about 30 minutes, until the custards are just set. (Push the point of a knife into the centre of one; if it comes out clean, the custards are cooked.) Remove from the pan, cool, then chill.

5 Preheat the grill (broiler). Sprinkle the sugar evenly over the surface of the custards and grill (broil) for 30–60 seconds, until the sugar melts and caramelizes, taking care not to let it burn. Place in the refrigerator to chill and set the crust.

COOK'S TIP

It is best to make the custards the day before you wish to eat them and chill overnight, so that they are really cold and firm.

Meringue Pyramid with Chocolate Mascarpone

This impressive cake makes a perfect centrepiece for the dinner table. Dust the pyramid with a little sifted icing (confectioners') sugar and sprinkle with just a few rose petals for simple but stunning presentation.

SERVES ABOUT TEN

200g/7oz plain (semisweet) chocolate

4 egg whites

150g/5oz/¾ cup caster (superfine) sugar

115g/4oz/½ cup mascarpone cheese

1 Preheat the oven to 150°C/300°F/Gas 2. Line two large baking sheets with baking parchment or greaseproof (waxed) paper. Grate 75g/3oz of the chocolate.

2 Whisk the egg whites in a clean, grease-free bowl until they form stiff peaks. Gradually whisk in half the sugar, then add the rest and whisk until the meringue is very stiff and glossy. Add the grated chocolate and whisk lightly to mix.

3 Draw a 20cm/8in circle on the lining paper on one of the baking sheets, turn it upside down, and spread the marked circle evenly with about half the meringue. Spoon the remaining meringue in 28–30 teaspoonfuls on both baking sheets. Bake the meringue for 1–1½ hours, or until crisp and completely dried out.

4 Make the filling. Melt the remaining chocolate in a heatproof bowl over hot water. Cool slightly, then stir in the mascarpone. Cool the mixture until firm.

5 Spoon the chocolate mixture into a large piping (pastry) bag and use to sandwich the meringues together in pairs, reserving a small amount of filling for the pyramid.

6 Peel off the baking parchment from the large round of meringue, then arrange the filled meringues on top, piling them up in a pyramid. Keep them in position with a few well-placed dabs of the reserved filling.

COOK'S TIP

The meringues can be made up to a week in advance and stored in a cool, dry place in an airtight container.

Chilled Chocolate and Espresso Mousse

Heady, aromatic espresso coffee adds a distinctive flavour to this smooth, rich mousse. For a special after dinner treat, serve the mousse in stylish chocolate cups decorated with sprigs of mint, with mascarpone or clotted cream on the side.

SERVES FOUR

450g/1lb plain (semisweet) chocolate

45ml/3 tbsp freshly brewed espresso

25g/1oz/2 tbsp unsalted (sweet) butter

4 eggs, separated

1 For each chocolate cup, cut a double thickness 15cm/6in square of foil. Mould it around a small orange, leaving the edges and corners loose to make a cup shape. Remove the orange and press the bottom of the foil case gently on a surface to make a flat base. Repeat to make four foil cups.

2 Break half the chocolate into small pieces and place in a bowl set over a pan of very hot water. Stir occasionally until the chocolate has completely melted.

3 Spoon the chocolate into the foil cups, spreading it up the sides with the back of a spoon to give a ragged edge. Chill for 30 minutes in the refrigerator, or until set hard. Gently peel away the foil, starting at the top edge.

4 To make the chocolate mousse, put the remaining chocolate and espresso into a bowl set over a pan of hot water and melt as before, until smooth and liquid. Stir in the butter, a little at a time. Remove the pan from the heat and then stir in the egg yolks.

5 Whisk the egg whites in a bowl until stiff, but not dry, then fold them into the chocolate mixture. Pour into a bowl and chill for at least 3 hours, or until the mousse is set. Scoop the chilled mousse into the chocolate cups just before serving.

Passion Fruit Creams

These delicately perfumed creams are light with a fresh flavour from the passion fruit. Ripe passion fruit should look purple and wrinkled – choose fruit that are heavy for their size. When halved, the fragrant, sweet juicy flesh with small edible black seeds are revealed. These creams can be decorated with mint or geranium leaves and served with cream.

SERVES FIVE TO SIX

1 Preheat the oven to 180°C/350°F/Gas 4. Line the bases of six 120ml/4fl oz/½ cup ramekins with rounds of baking parchment and place them in a roasting pan.

2 Heat the cream to just below boiling point, then remove the pan from the heat. Sieve (strain) the flesh of four passion fruits and beat together with the sugar and eggs. Whisk in the hot cream and then ladle into the ramekins.

3 Half fill the roasting pan with boiling water. Bake the creams for 25–30 minutes, or until set, then leave to cool before chilling.

4 Run a knife around the insides of the ramekins, then invert them on to serving plates, tapping the bases firmly. Carefully peel off the baking parchment and chill in the refrigerator until ready to serve. Spoon on a little passion fruit flesh just before serving.

600ml/1 pint/2½ cups double (heavy) cream, or a mixture of single (light) and double (heavy) cream

6 passion fruits

30–45ml/2–3 tbsp vanilla sugar

5 eggs

White Chocolate Castles

With a little ingenuity, good-quality bought ice cream can masquerade as a culinary masterpiece – it's down to perfect presentation. For a professional finish, dust the castles and plates with a hint of cocoa powder or icing (confectioners') sugar.

SERVES SIX

225g/8oz white chocolate, broken into pieces

250ml/8fl oz/1 cup white chocolate ice cream

250ml/8fl oz/1 cup dark chocolate ice cream

115g/4oz/1 cup berries

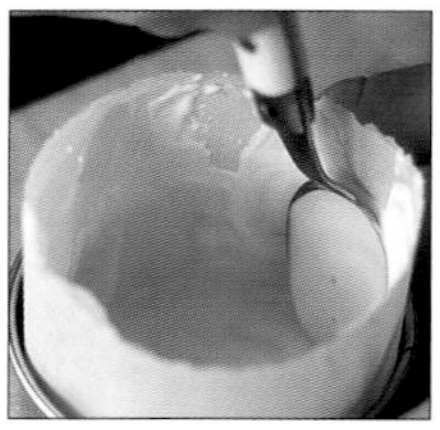

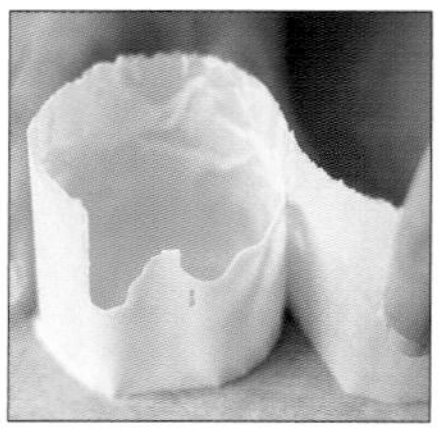

1 Put the white chocolate in a heatproof bowl, set it over a pan of gently simmering water and leave until melted. Line a baking sheet with greaseproof (waxed) paper. Cut out six 30 x 13cm/12 x 5in strips of greaseproof paper, then fold each in half lengthways.

2 Stand a 7.5cm/3in pastry (cookie) cutter on the baking sheet. Roll one strip of paper into a circle and fit inside the cutter with the folded edge on the base paper. Stick the edges together with tape.

3 Remove the cutter and shape more paper collars in the same way, leaving the pastry cutter in place around the final collar.

4 Spoon a little of the melted chocolate into the base of the collar supported by the cutter. Using a teaspoon, spread the chocolate over the base and up the sides of the collar, making the top edge uneven. Carefully lift away the cutter.

5 Make five more chocolate cases in the same way, using the cutter for extra support each time. Leave the cases in a cool place or in the refrigerator to set.

6 Carefully peel away the paper from the sides of the chocolate cases, then lift the cases off the base. Transfer to serving plates.

7 Using a large melon baller or teaspoon, scoop the white and dark chocolate ice creams into the cases and decorate with berries. Serve immediately.

Miniature Choc-ices

These little chocolate-coated ice creams make a fun alternative to the more familiar after-dinner chocolates, especially on hot summer evenings – although they need to be eaten quickly. Serve the choc-ices in fluted paper cases. If you can, buy gold cases as they will contrast very prettily with the dark chocolate coating.

MAKES ABOUT TWENTY-FIVE

750ml/1¼ pints/ 3 cups vanilla, chocolate or coffee ice cream

200g/7oz plain (semisweet) chocolate, broken into pieces

25g/1oz milk chocolate, broken into pieces

25g/1oz/¼ cup chopped hazelnuts, lightly toasted

1 Put a large baking sheet in the freezer for 10 minutes. Using a melon baller, scoop balls of ice cream and place these on the baking sheet. Freeze for at least 1 hour or until firm.

2 Line a second baking sheet with baking parchment and place in the freezer for 15 minutes. Melt the plain chocolate in a heatproof bowl set over a pan of gently simmering water. Melt the milk chocolate in a separate bowl.

3 Using a metal spatula, transfer the ice cream scoops to the parchment-lined sheet. Spoon a little plain chocolate over one scoop so that most of it is coated.

4 Sprinkle immediately with chopped nuts, before the chocolate sets. Coat half the remaining scoops in the same way, sprinkling each one with nuts before the chocolate sets. Spoon the remaining plain chocolate over all the remaining scoops.

5 Using a teaspoon, drizzle the milk chocolate over the choc-ices that are not topped with nuts. Freeze again until ready to serve.

Nutritional Information

The nutritional analysis below is **per portion**, unless otherwise stated. If the recipe gives a range, such as Serves 4–6, then the analysis will be for the smaller portion size, i.e. 6 servings. Measurements for sodium do not include salt added to taste.

p14 Spanish Salted Almonds Energy 206Kcal/853kJ; Protein 8g; Carbohydrate 2g, of which sugars 1g; Fat 19g, of which saturates 1g; Cholesterol 0mg; Calcium 80mg; Fibre 2.5g; Sodium 300mg.

p15 Polenta Chips Per chip: Energy 35Kcal/144kJ; Protein 1g; Carbohydrate 3g, of which sugars 0g; Fat 2g, of which saturates 1g; Cholesterol 4mg; Calcium 20mg; Fibre 0.1g; Sodium 100mg.

p16 Brandade of Salt Cod Energy 627Kcal/2583kJ; Protein 10g; Carbohydrate 1g, of which sugars 1g; Fat 64g, of which saturates 20g; Cholesterol 57mg; Calcium 96mg; Fibre 0.1g; Sodium 100mg.

p17 Baba Ghanoush Energy 395Kcal/1635kJ; Protein 13g; Carbohydrate 5g, of which sugars 4g; Fat 3g, of which saturates 5g; Cholesterol 0mg; Calcium 92mg; Fibre 8.1g; Sodium 100mg.

p18 Egg and Onion Topping Energy 245Kcal/1017kJ; Protein 12g; Carbohydrate 3g, of which sugars 2g; Fat 20g, of which saturates 5g; Cholesterol 389mg; Calcium 70mg; Fibre 0.5g; Sodium 200mg.

p18 Cheese with Green Olives Energy 252Kcal/1040kJ; Protein 4g; Carbohydrate 0g; Fat 26g, of which saturates 16g; Cholesterol 53mg; Calcium 116mg; Fibre 0.5g; Sodium 800mg.

p20 Bacon-rolled Enokitake Mushrooms Energy 116Kcal/483kJ; Protein 9g; Carbohydrate 1g, of which sugars 0g; Fat 9g, of which saturates 3g; Cholesterol 27mg; Calcium 10mg; Fibre 1.2g; Sodium 500mg.

p21 Spicy Chickpea Samosas Energy 580Kcal/2437kJ; Protein 20g; Carbohydrate 72g, of which sugars 12g; Fat 24g, of which saturates 6g; Cholesterol 17mg; Calcium 91mg; Fibre 8.3g; Sodium 500mg.

p22 Red Onion and Olive Pissaladière Energy 436Kcal/1815kJ; Protein 6g; Carbohydrate 37g, of which sugars 6g; Fat 31g, of which saturates 2g; Cholesterol 0mg; Calcium 77mg; Fibre 1.5g; Sodium 500mg.

p23 Potato and Onion Tortilla Energy 512Kcal/2132kJ; Protein 15g; Carbohydrate 40g, of which sugars 5g; Fat 34g, of which saturates 6g; Cholesterol 285mg; Calcium 73mg; Fibre 3.7g; Sodium 100mg.

p26 Avocado Soup Energy 301Kcal/1240kJ; Protein 4g; Carbohydrate 5g, of which sugars 3g; Fat 30g, of which saturates 12g; Cholesterol 45mg; Calcium 86mg; Fibre 2.5g; Sodium 600mg.

p27 Tuscan Bean Soup Energy 209Kcal/877kJ; Protein 8g; Carbohydrate 19g, of which sugars 9g; Fat 12g, of which saturates 2g; Cholesterol 0mg; Calcium 79mg; Fibre 6.6g; Sodium 500mg.

p28 Winter Squash Soup with Tomato Salsa Energy 255Kcal/1059kJ; Protein 3g; Carbohydrate 18g, of which sugars 12g; Fat 19g, of which saturates 3g; Cholesterol 0mg; Calcium 86mg; Fibre 3.1g; Sodium 100mg.

p29 Stilton and Watercress Soup Energy 162Kcal/671kJ; Protein 8g; Carbohydrate 1g, of which sugars 1g; Fat 14g, of which saturates 9g; Cholesterol 38mg; Calcium 169mg; Fibre 0.6g; Sodium 400mg.

p30 Curried Cauliflower Soup Energy 137Kcal/579kJ; Protein 11g; Carbohydrate 14g, of which sugars 12g; Fat 5g, of which saturates 2g; Cholesterol 11mg; Calcium 268mg; Fibre 2.3g; Sodium 200mg.

p31 Pea Soup with Garlic Energy 208Kcal/874kJ; Protein 14g; Carbohydrate 22g, of which sugars 6g; Fat 8g, of which saturates 4g; Cholesterol 13mg; Calcium 81mg; Fibre 11.7g; Sodium 700mg.

p32 Roast Asparagus with Crispy Prosciutto Energy 141Kcal/582kJ; Protein 7g; Carbohydrate 2g, of which sugars 2g; Fat 11g, of which saturates 3g; Cholesterol 18mg; Calcium 38mg; Fibre 1.5g; Sodium 400mg.

p33 Halloumi and Grape Salad Energy 274Kcal/1139kJ; Protein 10g; Carbohydrate 9g, of which sugars 9g; Fat 22g, of which saturates 10g; Cholesterol 14mg; Calcium 241mg; Fibre 0.6g; Sodium 1g.

p34 Cheese and Tomato Soufflés Energy 317Kcal/1319kJ; Protein 19g; Carbohydrate 6g, of which sugars 3g; Fat 25g, of which saturates 10g; Cholesterol 203mg; Calcium 395mg; Fibre 0.1g; Sodium 600mg.

p35 Tomato and Tapenade Tarts Energy 603Kcal/2512kJ; Protein 9g; Carbohydrate 50g, of which sugars 5g; Fat 43g, of which saturates 7g; Cholesterol 21mg; Calcium 117mg; Fibre 1.7g; Sodium 800mg.

p38 Stuffed Baby Squash Energy 469Kcal/1951kJ; Protein 14g; Carbohydrate 48g, of which sugars 1g; Fat 24g, of which saturates 10g; Cholesterol 36mg; Calcium 316mg; Fibre 2g; Sodium 300mg.

p39 Aubergines with Cheese Sauce Energy 509Kcal/2111kJ; Protein 22g; Carbohydrate 13g, of which sugars 7g; Fat 41g, of which saturates 19g; Cholesterol 80mg; Calcium 640mg; Fibre 2.2g; Sodium 900mg.

p40 Mushroom Polenta Energy 518Kcal/2155kJ; Protein 19g; Carbohydrate 46g, of which sugars 0g; Fat 26g, of which saturates 16g; Cholesterol 69mg; Calcium 333mg; Fibre 2.5g; Sodium 400mg.

p41 Roasted Peppers with Halloumi and Pine Nuts Energy 361Kcal/1504kJ; Protein 18g; Carbohydrate 16g, of which sugars 16g; Fat 26g, of which saturates 12g; Cholesterol 58mg; Calcium 105mg; Fibre 4.3g; Sodium 400mg.

p42 Roasted Aubergines with Feta and Coriander Energy 248Kcal/1028kJ; Protein 11g; Carbohydrate 3g, of which sugars 3g; Fat 21g, of which saturates 10g; Cholesterol 47mg; Calcium 252mg; Fibre 2.0g; Sodium 1g.

p43 Pasta with Roast Tomatoes and Goat's Cheese Energy 749Kcal/3156kJ; Protein 28g; Carbohydrate 95g, of which sugars 12g; Fat 31g, of which saturates 13g; Cholesterol 49mg; Calcium 419mg; Fibre 6.5g; Sodium 500mg.

p44 Crab Risotto Energy 345Kcal/1458kJ; Protein 20g; Carbohydrate 54g, of which sugars 0g; Fat 7g, of which saturates 1g; Cholesterol 54mg; Calcium 35mg; Fibre 0.3g; Sodium 900mg.

p45 Filo-wrapped Fish Energy 509Kcal/2135kJ; Protein 36.2g; Carbohydrate 37.2g, of which sugars 10.4g; Fat 25.1g, of which saturates 4.2g; Cholesterol 75mg; Calcium 137mg; Fibre 5g; Sodium 192mg.

p46 Haddock with Fennel Butter Energy 220Kcal/921kJ; Protein 29g; Carbohydrate 1g, of which sugars 1g; Fat 11g, of which saturates 7g; Cholesterol 81mg; Calcium 123mg; Fibre 0.3g; Sodium 200mg.

p47 Roast Cod Wrapped in Prosciutto with Vine Tomatoes Energy 342Kcal/1427kJ; Protein 38g; Carbohydrate 3g, of which sugars 3g; Fat 20g, of which saturates 4g; Cholesterol 98mg; Calcium 25mg; Fibre 1g; Sodium 400mg.

p50 Marinated Lamb with Oregano and Basil Energy 251Kcal/1042kJ; Protein 21g; Carbohydrate 0g; Fat 19g, of which saturates 5g; Cholesterol 67mg; Calcium 29mg; Fibre 0g; Sodium 1.2g.

p51 Beef Patties with Onions and Peppers Energy 339Kcal/1416 kJ; Protein 30g; Carbohydrate 15g, of which sugars 11g; Fat 18g, of which saturates 6g; Cholesterol 70mg; Calcium 60mg; Fibre 4.0g; Sodium 100mg.

p52 Meatballs in Tomato Sauce Energy 309Kcal/1290kJ; Protein 22g; Carbohydrate 12g, of which sugars 7g; Fat 20g, of which saturates 8g; Cholesterol 70mg;

Calcium 89mg; Fibre 2.0g; Sodium 800mg.
p53 Pancetta and Broad Bean Risotto Energy 526Kcal/2211kJ; Protein 18g; Carbohydrate 72g, of which sugars 4g; Fat 21g, of which saturates 6g; Cholesterol 29mg; Calcium 81mg; Fibre 3.4g; Sodium 2.4g.
p54 Paprika Pork Energy 249Kcal/1049kJ; Protein 31g; Carbohydrate 15g, of which sugars 8g; Fat 8g, of which saturates 2g; Cholesterol 88mg; Calcium 44mg; Fibre 3.0g; Sodium 300mg.
p55 Soy-marinated Chicken Energy 67Kcal/703kJ; Protein 34g; Carbohydrate 4g, of which sugars 3g; Fat 2g, of which saturates 0g; Cholesterol 88mg; Calcium 36mg; Fibre 1.7g; Sodium 500mg.
p56 Chicken Escalopes with Lemon and Serrano Ham Energy 253Kcal/1058kJ; Protein 36g; Carbohydrate 0g; Fat 12g, of which saturates 6g; Cholesterol 109mg; Calcium 9mg; Fibre 0g; Sodium 500mg.
p57 Roast Chicken with Herb Cheese, Chilli and Lime Stuffing Energy 220Kcal/921kJ; Protein 29g; Carbohydrate 0g; Fat 12g, of which saturates 6g; Cholesterol 131mg; Calcium 27mg; Fibre 0g; Sodium 200mg.
p58 Guinea Fowl with Whisky Sauce Energy 449Kcal/1866kJ; Protein 34g; Carbohydrate 1g, of which sugars 1g; Fat 29g, of which saturates 13g; Cholesterol 51mg; Calcium 56mg; Fibre 0g; Sodium 200mg.
p59 Duck with Plum Sauce Energy 334Kcal/1405kJ; Protein 33g; Carbohydrate 22g, of which sugars 21g; Fat 13g, of which saturates 4g; Cholesterol 144mg; Calcium 48mg; Fibre 2.8g; Sodium 100mg.
p62 Minty Broad Beans with Lemon Energy 118Kcal/493kJ; Protein 7g; Carbohydrate 9g, of which sugars 2g; Fat 7g, of which saturates 1g; Cholesterol 0mg; Calcium 35mg; Fibre 69g; Sodium 100mg.

p62 Gingered Carrot Salad Energy 82Kcal/339kJ; Protein 1g; Carbohydrate 7g, of which sugars 7g; Fat 7g, of which saturates 1g; Cholesterol 0mg; Calcium 70mg; Fibre 2.1g; Sodium 100mg.
p64 Asparagus with Lemon Sauce Energy 84Kcal/349kJ; Protein 6g; Carbohydrate 7g, of which sugars 4g; Fat 3g, of which saturates 1g; Cholesterol 90mg; Calcium 58mg; Fibre 2.9g; Sodium 100mg.
p65 Braised Lettuce and Peas with Spring Onions Energy 206Kcal/851kJ; Protein 8g; Carbohydrate 17g, of which sugars 8g; Fat 12g, of which saturates 7g; Cholesterol 27mg; Calcium 109mg; Fibre 6.5g; Sodium 100mg.
p66 Champ Energy 445Kcal/1858kJ; Protein 8g; Carbohydrate 49g, of which sugars 7g; Fat 25g, of which saturates 16g; Cholesterol 66mg; Calcium 143mg; Fibre 3.7g; Sodium 200mg.
p67 Asparagus, Bacon and Leaf Salad Energy 239Kcal/989kJ; Protein 13g; Carbohydrate 5g, of which sugars 5g; Fat 19g, of which saturates 4g; Cholesterol 19mg; Calcium 54mg; Fibre 2.7g; Sodium 800mg.
p68 Warm Chorizo and Spinach Salad Energy 273Kcal/1127kJ; Protein 8g; Carbohydrate 2g, of which sugars 2g; Fat 26g, of which saturates 6g; Cholesterol 0mg; Calcium 96mg; Fibre 1.2g; Sodium 300mg.
p69 Potato and Olive Salad Energy 296Kcal/1246kJ; Protein 5g; Carbohydrate 48g, of which sugars 4g; Fat 11g, of which saturates 2g; Cholesterol 0mg; Calcium 40mg; Fibre 3.3g; Sodium 300mg.
p72 Grilled Peaches with Meringues Energy 123Kcal/526kJ; Protein 2g; Carbohydrate 31g, of which sugars 31g; Fat 0g; Cholesterol 0mg; Calcium 24mg; Fibre 2.3g; Sodium 100mg.
p73 Apricot and Ginger Gratin Energy 414Kcal/1731kJ; Protein 4g; Carbohydrate 44g, of which sugars 35g; Fat 26g, of which saturates 16g; Cholesterol 48mg; Calcium 94mg; Fibre 2.4g; Sodium 200mg.
p74 Baked Ricotta Cakes with Red Sauce Energy 176Kcal/741kJ; Protein 8g; Carbohydrate 21g, of which sugars 21g; Fat 7g, of which saturates 4g; Cholesterol 31mg; Calcium 173mg; Fibre 1.4g; Sodium 100mg.
p75 Hot Blackberry and Apple Soufflé Energy 128Kcal/543kJ; Protein 2g; Carbohydrate 31g, of which sugars 31g; Fat 0g; Cholesterol 0mg; Calcium 28mg; Fibre 2.2g; Sodium 100mg.
p76 Treacle Tart Energy 416Kcal/1749kJ; Protein 4g; Carbohydrate 66g, of which sugars 35g; Fat 17g, of which saturates 0g; Cholesterol 0mg; Calcium 46mg; Fibre 1.3g; Sodium 300mg.
p77 Hot Chocolate Rum Soufflés Energy 91Kcal/382kJ; Protein 4g; Carbohydrate 12g, of which sugars 11g; Fat 2g, of which saturates 1g; Cholesterol 0mg; Calcium 14mg; Fibre 1.0g; Sodium 100mg.
p78 Caramelized Upside-down Pear Pie Energy 322Kcal/1347kJ; Protein 1g; Carbohydrate 37g, of which sugars 25g; Fat 20g, of which saturates 7g; Cholesterol 31mg; Calcium 18mg; Fibre 0.8g; Sodium 100mg.
p80 Blueberry and Almond Tart Energy 316Kcal/1324kJ; Protein 6g; Carbohydrate 41g, of which sugars 23g; Fat 16g, of which saturates 0g; Cholesterol 0mg; Calcium 41mg; Fibre 1.5g; Sodium 100mg.
p81 Baked Bananas with Ice Cream and Toffee Sauce Energy 368Kcal/1545kJ; Protein 4g; Carbohydrate 55g, of which sugars 52g; Fat 16g, of which saturates 10g; Cholesterol 40mg; Calcium 81mg; Fibre 1.1g; Sodium 400mg.
p84 Lemon Sorbet Energy 135Kcal/577kJ; Protein 1g; Carbohydrate 35g, of which sugars 35g; Fat 0g; Cholesterol 0mg; Calcium 6mg; Fibre 0g; Sodium 100mg.
p85 Strawberry and Lavender Sorbet Energy 123Kcal/522kJ; Protein 1g; Carbohydrate 31g, of which sugars 31g; Fat 0g; Cholesterol 0mg; Calcium 16mg; Fibre 0.9g; Sodium 100mg.
p86 Kulfi Energy 334Kcal/1389kJ; Protein 14g; Carbohydrate 24g, of which sugars 24g; Fat 20g, of which saturates 10g; Cholesterol 53mg;

Calcium 455mg; Fibre 0.6g; Sodium 200mg.
p87 Caramel and Pecan Terrine Energy 553Kcal/2292kJ; Protein 2g; Carbohydrate 27g, of which sugars 27g; Fat 49g, of which saturates 26g; Cholesterol 103mg; Calcium 46mg; Fibre 0.6g; Sodium 100mg.
p88 Baked Custard with Burnt Sugar Energy 992Kcal/4099kJ; Protein 6g; Carbohydrate 31g, of which sugars 31g; Fat 95g, of which saturates 57g; Cholesterol 430mg; Calcium 114mg; Fibre 0g; Sodium 100mg.
p89 Meringue Pyramid with Chocolate Mascarpone Energy 216Kcal/907kJ; Protein 3g; Carbohydrate 28g, of which sugars 28g; Fat 11g, of which saturates 7g; Cholesterol 12mg; Calcium 20mg; Fibre 0.5g; Sodium 100mg.
p90 Chilled Chocolate and Espresso Mousse Energy 710Kcal/2974kJ; Protein 13g; Carbohydrate 71g, of which sugars 70g; Fat 43g, of which saturates 24g; Cholesterol 253mg; Calcium 74mg; Fibre 2.8g; Sodium 100mg.
p91 Passion Fruit Creams Energy 602Kcal/2487kJ; Protein 8g; Carbohydrate 10g, of which sugars 10g; Fat 59g, of which saturates 35g; Cholesterol 330mg; Calcium 81mg; Fibre 0.5g; Sodium 100mg.
p92 White Chocolate Castles Energy 352Kcal/1476kJ; Protein 6g; Carbohydrate 43g, of which sugars 42g; Fat 18g, of which saturates 11g; Cholesterol 22mg; Calcium 198mg; Fibre 0.5g; Sodium 100mg.
p93 Miniature Choc-ices Energy 106Kcal/442kJ; Protein 2g; Carbohydrate 12g, of which sugars 11g; Fat 6g, of which saturates 3g; Cholesterol 8mg; Calcium 36mg; Fibre 0.3g; Sodium 100mg.

Index